79098
CT
524
.T8

# HEROES
# OF
# PUERTO RICO

*Foreword by The Honorable Herman Badillo
President, Borough of The Bronx*

# HEROES
# OF
# PUERTO RICO

by Jay Nelson Tuck
and
Norma Coolen Vergara

*in cooperation with*
Elsie E. González-Paz

*FLEET PRESS CORPORATION*
*New York/London*

© Copyright, 1969 Fleet Press Corporation
156 Fifth Avenue
New York City 10010

**All rights reserved**

Library of Congress Catalogue Card No. : 77-76027

SBN 8303-0070-8

No portion of this book may be reprinted, stored in an informational retrieval system, or transmitted, in any form or by any means, electronic, mechanical, photocopying, recording, or otherwise without the written permission of the publisher, except by a reviewer who wishes to quote brief passages in connection with a review for a newspaper, magazine, or radio-television program.

# ACKNOWLEDGEMENTS

No book of this kind is ever written by one person. Many hands and brains go into supplying the material from which it comes. By itself, the bibliography is a list of some of my debts, but there are many others. While I accept sole responsibility for any errors that may be found in the text, I wish to express my deep gratitude to Elsie E. González-Paz for contributing her awareness of the need for this book and valuable resource material; Tania Viera de Torres, Department of Education of Puerto Rico, for providing basic materials and important leads; the librarians of the Puerto Rican Information Office, New York City; the librarians of the New York Public Library's Bloomingdale, Central Circulation and Donnell branches; of the Greenwich, Connecticut library; and of the University of Connecticut; Anna Pacifica Vergara Coolen for many helpful translations of old Spanish terms and much essential information on Latin American customs and ways of life; Patricia Giles for diligent research and translation; Luis Muñoz Marín for checking the accuracy of the chapters about himself and his father; and to Dr. Morris Goodman for his patient and kindly help in more ways than I can enumerate.

It is conventional to end such acknowledgments as this with a bow to someone "without whose help this book would not have been possible". I say these words, not out of convention, but out of deepest gratitude: in the case of Norma Coolen Vergara Giles, it is literally true.

*Jay Nelson Tuck*

New York City
November, 1969

## *Names*

The Spanish custom holds in the matter of family names.

If a man's name is Juan González Ramírez, the González stands for his father and the Ramírez for his mother. He is addressed as Mr. González.

If Juan has a sister, María, she is María González Ramírez. If she marries Jorge García Velásquez, she continues to be María Gonzalez Ramírez but adds "de García Velásquez." You can address her as Mrs. García.

If she has a son, José, he is José García González.

# FOREWORD

It is often the case that a spokesman of a neighborhood or area may be highly regarded among his own, but he does not take on the aura of being a leader or hero until he receives recognition beyond his immediate community. Publication of a book is also considered a significant step in elevation. A book gives stature; it is official recognition. Just as an individual may gain higher status through recognition beyond his normal realm of activity, so can a nation or a people.

That is why I am so particularly pleased by the publication of *Heroes of Puerto Rico* in English. The leaders discussed are well known in Puerto Rico. Their lives and accomplishments are woven into the history, culture and folklore of the Island. To a certain extent, this has been carried over to the mainland where these leaders continue their following within Puerto Rican communities through the nation. However, almost all of the literature on leaders of Puerto Rico is in Spanish. Therefore, the knowledge of Puerto Rico's history, as told through its leaders, has been kept primarily to Spanish-speaking communities.

This means that this rich and brave heritage has been confined primarily to the Puerto Rican population itself. The Puerto Ricans are proud of their Island's history and background, but they have a perfect right to wonder who else knows about it. Youngsters, in particular, have a right to be annoyed that they learn about other lands and the heritage of their fellow classmates, but these other students do not study and get to know their Island's history.

The publication of *Heroes of Puerto Rico* will have a major effect in two areas—among the Puerto Rican youngsters both on the Island and here on the mainland, and among the rest of the nation's school population.

Among the Puerto Ricans, this long-overdue book will be a source of pride. It will mean, in effect, that they and their heritage are being recognized. Their leaders and their Island's history will be brought to the attention of their fellow classmates. It is quite common now for the history of Puerto Rico to be covered in classrooms on the mainland. But with the absence of a suitable textbook, it is studied in a special or different method, thereby giving the coverage a second-class status. This can now be ended.

However, I feel that the effect on the non-Puerto Rican students will be even greater. Through this book, these students can easily learn about Puerto Rico's history and heritage. The background of Puerto Rico can now be studied in the same way that the history of European or Asian countries is covered. On an individual basis, I believe this book will enable non-Puerto Rican youngsters to better understand their classmates who are of Puerto Rican origin or background.

The history of the struggle for freedom and identification in Puerto Rico is very similar to that of the United States and many other newer nations of the world. Therefore, these similarities will aid a better understanding among non-Puerto Ricans of Puerto Rico and its people.

The chapters on the battle for freedom from slavery and equal treatment for all are of particular significance. It will present an example of how one community faced the problems of a population of different backgrounds.

I hope *Heroes of Puerto Rico* will open a new phase in the study of Puerto Rico. This can lead to a fulfillment of the educational process, increased pride among youngsters of Puerto Rican origin and improved understanding among youngsters of different backgrounds.

Herman Badillo
*President*
*Borough of the Bronx*
*City of New York*

*New York City*
*October, 1969*

# CONTENTS

| | | |
|---|---|---|
| I | The Beginning | 13 |
| II | I Am Not Spanish—I am Puerto Rican!<br>Ramón Power Giralt | 19 |
| III | Black Children are not Admitted<br>Rafael Cordero y Molina | 31 |
| IV | I Wish to Become Someone<br>Román Baldorioty de Castro | 36 |
| V | The Man Who Bought Babies<br>Ramón Emeterio Betances y Alarcón | 46 |
| VI | The Emancipator<br>Segundo Ruiz Belvis | 55 |
| VII | The Man Who Never Gave Up<br>Ramón Marín Solá | 63 |
| VIII | Revolutions are Won by Ideas—Not by Hatred<br>Eugenio María de Hostos | 73 |
| IX | With Broken Wings . . . I Will Arrive<br>Luis Muñoz Rivera | 84 |

| | | |
|---|---|---|
| X | Black! Black! Black! I Am Proud of Being Negro! | |
| | José Celso Barbosa | 99 |
| XI | Rise Up! Revolt! Resist! | |
| | José de Diego y Martinez | 110 |
| XII | Hope Moves the People | |
| | Luis Muñoz Marín | 114 |
| | Bibliography | 137 |
| | Index | 139 |

# *HEROES*
## *OF*
## *PUERTO RICO*

# CHAPTER I

## THE BEGINNING

In the sparkling, deep-blue waters of the Caribbean Sea lies an emerald jewel. It is an island about 100 miles long and 35 miles across, and it is located about 1,000 miles southeast of Florida. Around its outer rim, whitecapped waves wash white sandy beaches, and palm trees wave gracefully in the breezes. Along the coastline, fruits, vegetables, tobacco and sugar cane grow in the rich earth. In the interior, oddly-shaped, green-covered mountains shoot up sharply to the blue sky. The island may well be one of the most beautiful places in the world.

Five hundred years ago, 15,000 Indians—most of them a tribe called Arawaks—lived there peacefully. The men hunted and fished while their wives gathered the fruits and tended the fields. They called the island Borinquén.

On November 19, 1493, some of those Indians looked out to sea and saw a strange and astonishing sight—one they had never seen before. Coming towards them were vessels bigger than they had known existed, above whose decks there rose towering masts and huge sheets of canvas spread like the white wings of great birds. Christopher Columbus, with seventeen ships and 1,500 men, landed on the island during his second voyage of discovery. No one knows the exact point at which he landed, and several towns today claim the honor of being the place. All over the island now there are statues of *Cristóbal Colón*, as his name is said in Spanish, usually in a heroic pose with his arms outstretched. It is an island joke that he is pointing into the distance and saying, "I landed over there."

Columbus landing at Hispaniola

Columbus named the island *San Juan Bautista*—St. John the Baptist—but as time went on it became known by the name of its most important harbor, Puerto Rico—the rich port—while the port itself became San Juan. Nobody is sure exactly when and how the island and the city exchanged names.

Traveling with Columbus was a young Spanish officer named Ponce de León, and he fell in love with Puerto Rico. Well he might, too, and not only for the great beauty of the place but for its people as well. In a letter to King Ferdinand and Queen Isabella back in Spain, Columbus described the people of a nearby island, but he might as well have been speaking of the Puerto Ricans when he said, "They are such a loving and generous people that I assure Your Highnesses there are no better people or land in the world. They love their neighbors as themselves, and their speech is the sweetest and gentlest in the world, and they always speak with a smile." He claimed the island for Spain.

Ponce loved the island so much that he came back 15 years later in 1508 to become the first Spanish Governor. Like colonialists everywhere, the Spanish quickly took over the best lands and set the Arawaks to working on the farms for them and panning the

Ponce de Leon

streams for gold. Ponce and some other Spaniards sent home for their families. He built a house for his wife and four children in Caparra, not far from what is now downtown San Juan. Then the place was a swamp, and the house was overrun with huge ants. Ponce's family had to set the feet of their beds in cans of water so the ants couldn't climb up the legs of the beds at night and bite the sleeping people.

Ponce did not stay very long. In 1513, as a result of politics in Spain, Diego Colón, Columbus' son, was named to succeed him as Governor. Ponce sailed west and discovered Florida. Thus, the wits say, he was the first Puerto Rican to come to the United States.

Ponce is said to have been a good and kind man, but not all of the Spanish rulers were. They were conquerors, and they behaved like conquerors, forcing the Indians to work for them, taking the prettiest Indian women for themselves, and punishing cruelly anyone who disobeyed them. They soon found out that growing sugar was profitable, but there were not enough Indians to cut all the cane they wanted to grow. This is why the Spaniards began to import black slaves from Africa, and by 1550 there were 15,000 of them on the island.

San Juan as it looked in the 17th Century

Sometimes slaves would escape from their owners. Back in the mountains and rain forest of the interior of the island, they could not be found. There they could clear a patch of land, build a cabin and live without fear. Indians and Spaniards who wanted to escape to freedom also fled into the hills. Over the centuries these people intermarried. Their descendants are the *jíbaros*—the word means "country people"—of today, still tough and independent beneath their gentleness and courtesy.

There were constant wars and revolutions in the countries around Puerto Rico, and so crowds of refugees from other lands would frequently arrive. The island's bays and rivers offered convenient hiding places for the pirates who sailed the Spanish Main, and who often robbed the natives. The evil Captain Kidd visited Puerto Rico, and there are legends today that some of his treasure is still buried there.

The Spanish ruled that Puerto Rico could trade only with Spain and that all goods must be carried in Spanish ships. Naturally, such an unfair rule caused smuggling to spring up and flourish, principally between the island and the American colonies. (Smuggling is secretly taking goods into or out of a country.)

The Great Seal of Puerto Rico

Puerto Rico was not so valuable to the Spanish for its treasures. The gold which the first conquerors had found was soon gone, and, despite the sugar trade, the island remained poor. What was important was its location as a gateway to Spain's other New World colonies. (That same location was to make the island important to the United States centuries later as a place from which the Panama Canal could be protected.)

Other countries wanted Puerto Rico for reasons similar to Spain's. As a result, the little island was repeatedly raided and invaded, but in the end she always fought off her attackers, though often with much suffering. Puerto Rico suffered from still another enemy—hurricanes that sometimes swept over her, smashing houses, destroying whole towns, bringing disease, death and homelessness to the people.

But most of all, she suffered under Spanish rulers. The people had no rights. The Governor, appointed from Madrid, had great powers. He headed the police. He made the laws. He decided who was guilty of breaking them. He fixed all punishments, including death. He could interfere with the affairs of the church. A Puerto Rican could not even travel from one village to another without the Governor's permission, and the Governor could order anyone where to live. The Puerto Ricans called this kind of government tyranny or oppression.

The people could not even buy or sell such necessities of life as clothing, tools, paper, flour and oil except from Spaniards who charged what they pleased. They had no voice whatever in their government. As one historian said, the people had "to endure men who are used to command with heat and to be obeyed in silence."

Small wonder that the Puerto Ricans longed for freedom! Small wonder that after hundreds of years of such oppression, one of the island's great poets, Lola Rodríguez de Tío, would say:

"I am not an enemy of Spain, but only of those unfeeling Spaniards who wish to rule over us with an iron hand. Such people have no love, either for us or for Spain, because, in the name of Spain and of God, they come here to commit acts of tyranny. Of such as these, yes, I am an enemy!"

And so was Ramón Power Giralt, the first of the great heroes of Puerto Rico's long struggle for liberty.

## CHAPTER II

### "I AM NOT SPANISH—I AM PUERTO RICAN!"

To a boy of the 18th Century, there was probably nothing quite so wonderful in all the world as a ship. Yet in those days many a boy grew up to manhood inland and then became old and died, having heard stories about ships all his life, but never having seen one.

Ramón Power Giralt was luckier than the average boy. He was born on October 27, 1775, in San Juan, Puerto Rico's capital city and greatest port. As a lad, he could see tall ships sailing in and out of the harbor in all their majesty. Walking along the waterfront, he could listen to the sailors' tales of strange, far-off places and thrill to their stories of fearful storms and wrecks. Ramoncito (little Ramón) dreamed of going to sea.

Ramón's parents were of proud, old Spanish families. His father, Don Joaquin Power y Morgan, was born in Bilbao, and his mother, Doña María Josefa Giralt Santaelle, in Barcelona—both ancient cities in Spain. Don Joaquin was an officer in the government which ruled Puerto Rico for the King of Spain. His post was in the City of San Juan, and he had the title of *Teniente Real*, meaning Royal Lieutenant.

When Ramón was still quite small, the thirteen American colonies declared their independence from the Mother Country, England, and the Revolution or War for Independence began. Spain took sides with the American colonists and made several loans of money to them. This war stirred up great excitement in the colonies of other nations in the New World. The colonists began to feel that if the North Americans could fight mighty

England for freedom, the Latin Americans could hope for freedom from Spain, too.

In Spanish-speaking countries the men sit around the dinner table until late talking, usually about politics. When they are old enough to behave, the boys are occasionally allowed to stay with the men. Sometimes they may even try out their own young opinions if what they say is bright and short. Ramón must have heard much talk of the Revolution taking place on the mainland.

He certainly must have heard of the exciting time when two American ships, chased by a British warship, took refuge in the Puerto Rican harbor of Mayagüez. There the *Mayagüeños*—the people of the city—ran their own flag up the masts of the ships to fool the British who could not then tell which vessels were the American ones. We know that later on Power read deeply the writings of some of the American Revolutionists—such as Thomas Paine, James Madison, Alexander Hamilton and Thomas Jefferson—and that he was much influenced by their ideas on liberty.

There were almost no schools in Puerto Rico when Ramón was growing up. The children of rich people were usually taught at home for a few years and then were sent to schools in Spain. Poor children received no schooling at all. When Ramón was twelve, and his brother, José, was fourteen, their father decided it was time for them to go to Spain.

They sailed on a frigate—a kind of big warship—named *Esperanza*, which means *Hope*. What an opportunity for a boy who meant to be a ship's captain someday! During the weeks of the long voyage, he had a chance to poke about every part of the vessel, to ask endless questions of her crew, to see how everything was done. It is safe to say that *Esperanza* had no secrets from the bright, curious boy by the time the voyage ended.

It almost ended sadly. A fierce storm broke when the ship was near the Spanish coast, and *Esperanza* very nearly sank. The ship was in such danger that sailors from the port of Castro set out in small boats to save the passengers. The Power boys were ordered to leave the ship and jump into a boat. Just as Ramón leaped, a huge wave heaved the boat up and away from the ship, and the boy fell into the roaring sea. A seaman leaned halfway out of the boat, strong hands gripped Ramón, and strong arms pulled him aboard. Today in the Church of San José in San Juan there hangs a painting of the rescue by the famous Puerto Rican painter, José Campeche.

The French Revolution was going on while Ramón was in Europe, but in spite of that he went to France, to the cities of Bordeaux and Bayonne, for part of his education. While he was there, the slaves of Haiti, a French colony not far from Puerto Rico, staged a bloody revolution of their own. Letters from home must have told Power about the horrors occuring in Haiti and of the desperate refugees who escaped and were arriving by ship in Puerto Rico. Halfway through his teens Ramón Power knew more about the struggle for liberty than most people learn in a lifetime.

Ramón Power

At the age of seventeen, Ramón returned from France to Spain and entered the Coast Guard Academy at Cádiz. He was an excellent student, and on May 23, 1793, he was graduated and became an officer in the navy. He did well in several sea battles and won rapid promotion.

In 1801, he was given a year's leave and returned to Puerto Rico, to rest and enjoy himself. The handsome young officer in his brilliant uniform was invited to many parties and balls, but he did not spend much time having fun. Power was deeply shocked at the conditions he found in his homeland. He traveled from one end of the island to the other, his own heart torn by the poverty, hunger and hopelessness of his people. Within him rose a deep anger that was never to die.

He spent so much time investigating everything that his brother, José, asked him why he was doing it. Ramón answered, "Because I know deep down inside me that some day I will have to give all my strength to the liberation of this island."

When his leave was up, Power returned to the Spanish navy. He was captain of *El Cometa—The Comet*—so named because she was a very fast ship. The ship was assigned to carry mail between Spain and the Americas, so Power visited many New World countries. During the long weeks at sea, as he walked the deck and listened to the creak of the masts, the flap of the sails and the slap of the waves against the ship, he had plenty of time to think about the relationship between the two worlds that were linked by his ship.

Now Power saw something of a revolution for himself. Some years earlier Spain had been forced to give up to France possession of Santo Domingo, an island near Puerto Rico. Now France had invaded Spain, and the Dominicans rose in revolt against the French on their island. Puerto Rico's Spanish government of course sympathized with the revolutionaries. Power was ordered to take a small fleet of Spanish warships to Santo Domingo to keep French reinforcements out. Once again he did his job well, and he won important victories.

Meanwhile, in faraway places, the stage was being set for his greatest adventure. Spain was hard-pressed by the French and wanted to keep her colonies on her side. To insure the loyalty of the Puerto Ricans, the Spanish government decided to allow the island to elect one Deputy to the *Cortes*, the Spanish parliament, which was somewhat like the United States Congress, but with different powers.

Spain also sent a new Governor to the island. On June 30, 1809, the ship *Penelope* sailed into San Juan harbor bringing Brigadier Don Salvador Meléndez Bruna, who was greeted with the firing of cannon, parades and the raising of flags. He was given the keys of the city and a feast in *la Fortaleza* (the Fortress), which was then and still is the Governor's official house.

La Fortaleza, San Juan Bay

Meléndez was a snob—a person who looked down on others for reasons having nothing to do with their real worth as people. He thought no native-born Puerto Rican was as good as anyone born in Spain. He could not understand why a man like Power would say proudly to himself, "I am not a Spaniard. I am a Puerto Rican." Furthermore, Power was known throughout the island for having spoken and written in favor of changes which the Governor and other upper-class Spaniards did not want.

Meléndez and other Governors before and after him got rich by stealing public money. Power wrote to a friend, "The Governor says, for example, that he has bought 1,000 barrels of flour for 18 *pesos* each when actually they cost only 15 *pesos*. They are charged to the public at 18 *pesos*, and the seller is given 18,000 *pesos*, but then he hands 3,000 *pesos* back to the Governor. The situation smelled so bad at one time that the Ministers in Spain got wind of it and ordered free trade in flour. But the order was never carried out because this graft was considered overtime pay for the Governors! "

One of the worst laws forced every farmer on the island to give some of his cattle to the government in San Juan. Power said, "The law ordered that every farmer send one out of every six head of cattle he owned, or even one out of every four, to the capital. He was obliged to deliver it, no matter how far the distance. His was the risk and the loss if the animal died or got lost on the way. Even the poor farmer who owned only one cow to help feed his small children or but one pair of oxen to help work the small farm that was his livelihood was not spared, for the selfish people ignored the cries of the poor who were robbed."

It's not surprising that the Governors of Puerto Rico did not like the man who kept calling attention so forcefully to their crimes!

Fifteen days after Meléndez' arrival, the *Junta Electoral* (Electoral Council) met in *la Fortaleza* to choose Puerto Rico's Deputy to the *Cortes*. To Meléndez's disgust, the man chosen was Ramón Power Giralt who wasn't even there, being off on his ship fighting the French.

Power returned to San Juan and received a true hero's welcome. He rode in a parade under arches of flowers. There were parties, the singing of hymns, and there were speeches and fireworks. The Puerto Rican people hoped that Power might be the person who would bring them some measure of liberty.

People from every corner of the island told Power what they wanted: schools and hospitals, a special school where juvenile delinquents could be taught a trade "because laws which prevent crime are far better than laws which punish it". They wanted Puerto Ricans to get the good government jobs which were filled by Spaniards and better roads and bridges "because the ones we have are so bad and dangerous that they are more fit for birds than for men".

Their other demands were the following: A university should be established. Idle land owned by the government should be distributed to farmers. The tax system should be improved. Puerto Rico should be allowed to trade freely with her neighbors. Working men should be allowed to have trade unions. Law officers should be elected, not appointed by the Governor.

On the morning of August 16, 1809, Power went to the Cathedral in San Juan to receive the blessings of his church on his

Bishop Juan Alejo de Arizmendi

journey. The highest officials, including Governor Meléndez, were there, while the plain people filled the great church to its walls. Leading the assembled priests was Bishop Don Juan Alejo de Arizmendi, who, like Power, was native-born. Standing beside his fellow *puertorriqueño*, the Bishop began a formal speech. Then, overcome by his feelings, he stopped.

In silence, he took from his finger the episcopal ring, the mark of his high church office. Taking Power's hand in his own, he placed the ring on the finger of the new Deputy. "This," he said, "is to remind you always to keep firm your resolve to protect the rights of our countrymen."

Men and women wept openly. It is perhaps as well that the thoughts of Governor Meléndez are not recorded. Although we do not know what he thought, we do know what he did. He tried in every possible way to prevent Power from carrying out his duties. Though earlier he had admitted that Power had been properly elected Deputy, he now wrote to the Spanish government saying the election had not been proper, and Power should not be allowed to go to Spain. He tried in every way to delay Power's travel arrangements. He fought against Power's choice of Don Estéban de Ayála for his secretary. He blocked payment of Power's salary.

However, his dirty tricks failed. He succeeded only in delaying Power's departure until the following April. At last Power and Don Estéban were on their way! They sailed for Cádiz where the *Cortes* was to meet.

While their ship was at sea, revolution against the Spanish government broke out in Venezuela. In Puerto Rico, Governor Meléndez at once sent off a fleet of seven ships, bearing 1,000 men, to help the Spanish in Venezuela crush the people. The sympathies of the Puerto Rican people, naturally, were with the people of Venezuela.

While Power waited in Cádiz for the *Cortes* to meet, he was horrified to learn that the Spanish government issued a Royal Order giving Meléndez "omnipotent powers" in Puerto Rico "so that he might keep his island free of the Venezuelan contagion". (A contagion is a sickness that one person can catch from another, and the Spanish did not want the Puerto Ricans to "catch" a taste for freedom.) "Omnipotent powers" meant that Meléndez could do anything he wanted to do. He could seize any property, arrest any person, imprison or put him to death, without any trial without even letting anybody know what he was doing. No wonder that Power resolved that the first thing he must do was to get that Royal Order repealed!

Despite his new powers, Meléndez could not keep the Puerto Rican people from sympathizing with the Venezuelans. Six young Venezuelans who had been studying to become priests came to San Juan. Meléndez directly ordered Bishop Arizmendi not to ordain them—swear them in as priests officially. Arizmendi ignored the order and ordained the young men. Meléndez did not dare take action directly against the beloved Bishop, but he ordered the six young priests to leave the island.

The Spanish sent a man named Antonio Cortabarría to Puerto Rico as Royal Commissioner to solve the Venezuelan problem. Cortabarría planned to draft Puerto Ricans into an army to fight the Venezuelan revolutionaries. But he woke one morning to find that during the night someone had nailed a paper to his door, saying, "Our people shall never permit the removal of a single American from this island to take him to fight against his brothers in Venezuela." Cortabarría decided that he had better not be too tough with the Puerto Ricans, though Meléndez, in revenge, did take some poor victims from his jails and send them off to Venezuela.

Meanwhile, the islanders were waiting anxiously for news from Spain. What would Power be able to do in the *Cortes*? Would the *Cortes* even listen to him? He was, after all, only one Deputy among many.

The first news came. The *Cortes* was meeting. The man who had been elected Vice President of the *Cortes* of 1810 was Ramón Power Giralt! Their Deputy! Puerto Rico would be heard! The islanders were wild with joy and hope.

Now news was awaited even more anxiously, if that were possible—news that might "break the chains which crush the people and keep them from advancing a single step". A writer of the day said, "A ship from Spain excites general joy which shows on everyone's face. Children urge their fathers out into the streets to find out the news. Crowds of people, wishful and happy, surround the captain. Newspapers are passed from hand to hand and much care is needed lest they get lost among so many begging hands."

In Cádiz, Power was fighting hard for the repeal of the Royal Order and for the removal of Meléndez. He told the *Cortes* that the Order was "barbaric, tyrannical, the most outrageous thing in the history of American oppression". He ripped into Meléndez, saying, "There are realms in which a Spanish citizen is not really free. In the blessed isle of Puerto Rico there are 200,000 loyal subjects who can be wiped out any time they should be unlucky enough to incur the hatred or dislike of the man who rules them."

Meléndez was really worried that Power might succeed in getting him fired. Power did get the Royal Order repealed, but Meléndez had a brother high in the Spanish government who blocked Power's efforts to have the Governor sent home to Spain.

When the news came through that he would remain in office, Meléndez shouted at a meeting of government officials, "The tyrant is alive again! I have fortresses and jails for everyone, and my whip is very long as you shall now see!" He tightened the screws on the people still more.

Letters of protest poured across the ocean to Power. Again and again he spoke in the *Cortes*. By the sheer justice of his cause and the force of his talk, he made the *Cortes* issue a series of orders to Meléndez. They ordered him to stop stealing Power's salary, to stop opening Power's mail, to change the tax on bread, and in various other ways to stop abusing his office.

Power spoke in the *Cortes*, not only for the people of Puerto Rico, but for all of the Spanish colonies. He warned Spain that if cruel oppression continued, people would revolt everywhere, and Spain would lose all her colonies. Several revolutions going on in Latin America gave sharp point to his words. "My profession has taken me to many places in both Americas," he said. "On these visits I have learned the hearts and opinion of their citizens. And in the Americas there are a few distinguished persons at the top and, at the bottom, a whole people complaining of being always ignored and treated with hurtful contempt."

Power won from the *Cortes* a ruling that gave all Spanish colonials equal rights with citizens born in Spain. Puerto Rico burst with joy when the news came. There were public demonstrations and feasts in all the towns. In San Juan there were fireworks, music in the town hall for three nights, and a solemn service of thanksgiving in the Cathedral.

Power also won a number of important reforms which together became known as the "Power Law". One of these created a new title in the government of Puerto Rico called the *Intendente* which was entirely separate from, and independent of, the Governor's office. The first *Intendente* was Don Alejandro Ramírez who was given authority over the business and trade of the island. Ramírez worked hard and honestly at trying to improve conditions in the island, and he did a good job. Among other things, he cracked down on smuggling from which many dishonest people had grown rich. By collecting the taxes on goods that had previously been smuggled, in one year alone he increased the income of the public treasury from 70,000 to 200,000 *pesos*.

Another reform of the Power Law created new seaports at the towns of Ponce, Aguadilla, Cabo Rojo and Fajardo. Until that time all shipping had been through San Juan, and the new ports helped business in other parts of the island.

The Power Law also started the delivery of mail all over the island, reduced high taxes on the necessities of life, wiped out taxes on imported flour and created the *Real Sociedad Económica de Amigos del País* (Royal Economic Society of the Friends of the Country), an organization which developed many new ways of improving life in Puerto Rico.

On March 19, 1812, Power scored a stunning victory. On that day the *Cortes* approved his proposal to give to Puerto Rico the first constitution ever won by any Spanish colony. The constitution declared the island to be no longer a colony, but a province of Spain, fully equal to any province in European Spain itself. Some Puerto Ricans of 25 or older were given the right to vote. All were guaranteed the right to think as they pleased, to work where they chose and to petition the government when they thought they were wronged. They were guaranteed that their homes could not be invaded, their property could not be seized, and they themselves could not be arrested unless they had committed crimes.

The news of the new constitution reached the island on July 9, and on July 14 the document became effective. The celebrations of that day put all previous ones to shame.

As in many other matters, the struggle for Puerto Rican liberty was a case of two steps forward, one step back. A later Spanish government wiped out the new constitution as well as other victories Power had won. But some of his reforms, including the Power Law, remained in effect to the lasting benefit of the people.

In the spring of 1813, an epidemic of yellow fever swept Cádiz, killing many people, including 30 Deputies to the *Cortes*. Among them was Ramón Power Giralt, who died on June 10, 1813. He was not yet 39 years of age. He and the 29 other Deputies were buried together in a single tomb that remains today as a monument to their loss.

## CHAPTER III

### "BLACK CHILDREN ARE NOT ADMITTED"

As the 18th Century drew to its close there were only two primary schools in all Puerto Rico—one in San Juan and one in San Germán. A little boy named Rafael Cordero wanted to go to the one in San Juan, but could not because the rule was: "Black children are not admitted."

Rafael could not understand why a child should be kept from getting an education because of the color of his skin. Even as a small boy, he made up his mind to do something about it, and he did. From the time when he was a very young man until his death—58 years in all—he ran a school and made welcome any child who wanted to come, no matter how poor he was, and no matter whether he was black, white or Indian. This gentle and good man became one of the most beloved of all Puerto Ricans. His countrymen called him *El Maestro*—The Teacher.

Rafael Cordero y Molina was born in San Juan in October, 1790. No one knows the exact day of his birth. His parents must have been people of education because they taught the boy to read and write. Little Rafael had a huge appetite for learning and read every book he could get his hands on. To earn a living, he also learned to be a shoemaker.

Being educated made Cordero a most unusual man in such a poor country. Besides the two primary schools that existed in 1797, there were a few secondary or high schools run by the Catholic Church, but they mainly taught subjects of interest to students who planned to become priests or nuns. Most people were so ignorant that they did not even know the numbers of the years. They would say that they had been born in the year that So-and-So became Governor, or had been married in the year of such-and-such a hurricane. They seemed to remember both Governors and hurricanes as disasters—each meant some kind of tragedy to the people.

The government just did not spend money for free schools. In 1799 the City Council of San Juan appointed four women to teach reading, writing and Christian principles. But in 1804 the Council still hadn't paid them their salary. Yet these four unselfish and dedicated ladies—María Dolores Araujo, Josefa Echevarría, Paula Molinero and Juana Polanco—had gone on teaching.

Even Meléndez, when he became Governor, was shocked by what he found. He wrote back to the Spanish government that he wanted to start some early schooling "because in this island there is hardly anyone who can read". He imported some books from Spain and had them reprinted in Puerto Rico to be sold at cost.

So the tiny school that Cordero opened in San Germán in 1810 was very badly needed. In one little house he had his living space, his shoemaker's workshop and his schoolroom. Cordero charged nothing for his teaching, and any child could come and be made welcome.

And they came—barefoot children from the farms and sugar cane fields, wearing perhaps only a ragged cotton shirt. They came when their families could spare them from work that even small children had to do. Boys carried seed and straw on the farms, or drove the teams of oxen. Girls who were old enough took care of the littler ones at home. Men worked all day long—14 or 15 hours—cutting cane under the broiling sun for a wage of a few cents. Often even that little money was not paid in cash, but in stamps which could be "spent" only at the plantation owner's store. This system not only forced the workers to pay high prices at the owner's store, but it also kept them from getting away because what little "money" they had was not good anywhere else. Even the work in the cane fields lasted only during the harvest season. For the rest of the year, many people had no work at all.

Then, as now, there were ignorant and unfeeling people who asked why the poor did not help themselves. They were people who did not see the plantation system at work, with its miserable housing, its big families crowded into a few feet of space without windows or chimneys.

Nor did the rich know what the poor knew all too well—what it feels like to be hungry. The poor rarely got enough of important kinds of food, such as milk to make good bones or meat to build strength. The *jíbaros* told a story about a man who sat down to his dinner and asked where the meat was. "It's right there," says his wife, pointing, "right behind that grain of rice."

Because of the poverty, food that left them weak, and the people's ignorance of how to take care of themselves, disease was everywhere. Most people never saw a doctor in their lives. Many died in childhood, and few lived to what we would now call middle age.

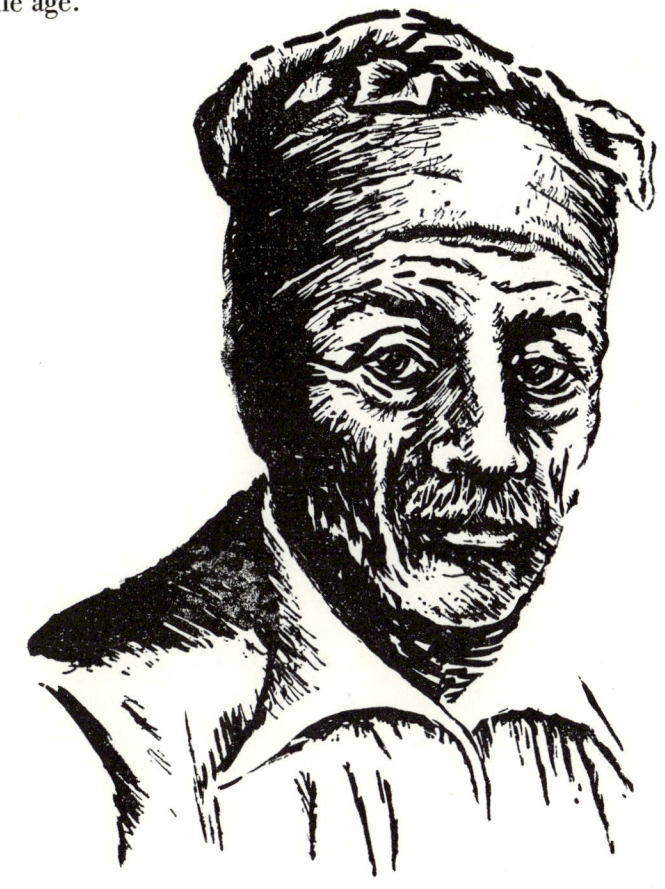

Rafael Cordero

Cordero saw all this with a sad heart. He welcomed children, especially the poor. No beggar ever left his house without food and a little money.

When we want to say that a man is especially generous, we sometimes say, "He would give you the shirt off his back." One time, as Cordero was sitting down to his lunch, a hungry beggar dressed in rags knocked at his door. Cordero invited the man in and gave him his own food. When the man had eaten, Cordero gave him one of his shirts, a pair of pants and a few coins. Then he made himself a meal of left-overs and went back to work.

He had not been teaching very long when his sister, Celestina, joined his school and began to teach the girls. After a few years, they moved from San Germán to San Juan, where Cordero had not been allowed in school. There they set up their home, the school and the shoemaker's workshop in a little house on the *Calle de la Luna* (Moon Street). The house is still there.

Cordero supported himself by making and repairing shoes and other odd jobs, never accepting a cent for his teaching. Among the pupils who formed their first ideas under his care were a number who went on to become great men. Román Baldorioty de Castro was perhaps the most famous, but there were several others who were almost as well known.

If someone praised Cordero's work, he would answer, "I cut the tree and my calloused hand carves it, but someone more able than I must finish it with beauty and brilliance." He meant that he could start his pupils in the right direction, but they themselves and the teachers who came after him were responsible for how far they went.

His modesty was extreme. Once a painter friend of his asked him to pose for a painting of himself. Cordero refused. The friend persisted, and finally Cordero agreed, but only on condition that the picture not be publicly shown until after he had died!

He always looked forward, never backward. Someone once asked him why he did not write about his work. He answered, "I write nothing in this life because I do not want to spend today remembering whatever good I did yesterday."

To Cordero, ignorance was a reproach to mankind, and hunger was a crime against humanity. It was his dream that an educated

Puerto Rico would wipe out hunger, poverty and tyranny. His was a vision that did not fail. He worked humbly and, in his simple way, he accomplished much. The future leaders he trained did help to improve all Puerto Rico, and he gave many unknown people the chance to improve their lives. The poet, José Gualberto Padilla, wrote that Cordero was "priest of the idea of the worker's education. The noble shoemaker had the faith that redeems and creates."

Cordero never sought help from the government for his work, and only near the end of his long life was he rewarded for it. The Economic Society of the Friends of the Country—the organization that was founded under the Power Law—gave him a Prize of Virtue, worth 100 *pesos*. Cordero divided the money equally, spending half on books and clothing for his pupils and distributing the rest among the beggars of San Juan. In his last years the Society also gave him a salary of 15 *pesos* a month.

In the summer of 1868, Don Rafael—then 78 years old—fell sick. Two officials came to see him. He turned to them in his pain and said:

"I understand that the hour of my death is near and that God is calling me. For the last eight days I have been unable to give classes. The children need the bread of the mind. And since I do not want what is not mine, deduct from my salary those eight days in which I have not fulfilled my duty. Look for another teacher to take my place and pray to God for my soul."

He died on July 5. The coffin was carried through the streets of San Juan on the shoulders of men he had taught. Behind it walked many hundreds of the people he would have wanted to be there—the poor of the city. Along the way, hundreds more knelt weeping in the streets, to say a prayer as he passed.

His house on Moon Street is kept today as a monument. But surely the monument that would have pleased him more is elsewhere, on Fernando Juncos Avenue in Santurce. It is a big and beautiful public school—the Rafael Cordero School.

All children are welcome there.

# CHAPTER IV

## "I WISH TO BECOME SOMEONE"

When young Román Baldorioty de Castro wrote in a letter to his brother, "I wish to become someone," he did not mean that he wanted to be a rich man. He was born poor, he lived simply all his life and when he died his friends had to collect money for his burial. But he certainly did become "someone". Luis Muñoz Rivera called him "the greatest man produced by this country".

Baldorioty was born on February 28, 1822, in a very poor home at Guaynabo. Not much is known about his parents, except that they were not married and that his mother was of Indian blood, or partly so. The neighborhood streets were his earliest school. There he learned to know hunger and illness, the lessons of the poor of Puerto Rico. He was a bright boy, and his mother wanted him to have an education. She knew that *El Maestro*, Rafael Cordero, would not turn away her boy. So the family moved to San Juan where young Román learned his letters and numbers at Cordero's school.

That school might have been the only one for the boy, but fortunately, *Padre* (Father) Rufo Manuel Fernandez heard about the bright lad, and took Román into his school, the only high school on the island. The boy became one of *Padre* Rufo's favorite pupils. After school, Román and another student, José Julián Acosta, took lessons in English and French at the *Sociedad Económica de Amigos del País*. They became two of the first four Puerto Rican boys to win scholarships for further education in Spain.

Unhappily, soon after they arrived in Spain the other two boys, Eduardo Micault and Julián Nuñez, fell desperately sick. Most people avoided those who were ill for fear of catching the disease themselves. They would stay at a distance and throw food to where the sick man could reach it. But Román nursed his schoolmates with loving devotion until they died, far from home. *Padre* Rufo, who had come to Spain with the boys, wrote the *Sociedad* about this good deed and won a reward for Román which enabled him to stay longer in Spain.

Step by step, Román was educated, never knowing how next year's learning could be paid for. He and Acosta finished their studies in Spain with excellent grades. But while they were there, the boys never forgot their own island. With Segundo Ruiz Belvis and Alejandro Tapia y Rivera, they founded a Society for the Collection of Historical Documents of the Island of San Juan Bautista of Puerto Rico. They worked to find and rescue important papers about Puerto Rico which might otherwise be lost forever in the dusty files of the Spanish government.

Román was given the chance to study further in Paris at the Central School of French Arts and Manufactures. In 1853, at the age of 31, he returned to Puerto Rico, now a full professor, able to teach in many branches of science. He began to teach and in 1854 became a professor at the new School of Commerce, Navigation and Agriculture in Ponce. His joy in his new job was dimmed only by the death of his beloved teacher and friend, *Padre* Rufo.

Just because his own life was going well did not mean that Baldorioty closed his eyes to other people's troubles. As he had as a little boy, he noticed everything. Watching the Spanish government of the island, he wrote, "The weight of great power crushes the goodness of the man who rules and the honesty of those who are ruled."

Watching the rich slaveowners, he wrote, "It is good to preserve the name, wealth and honors you inherit, but it is better in every way if you yourself create a position and a name. The first requires good sense, but the second demands will power and great virtue."

And looking at Puerto Rico as a whole, he said, "Our people lack unity and have no faith in themselves. The teachers, the

Román Baldorioty de Castro

workers, the artists, the industrialists, the farmers and the merchants are never joined together in a common thought. Selfishness forms the basis of our society."

These thoughts did not make him popular with the people whose wrong actions he was watching, but the poor Puerto Ricans and those who wanted good goverment began to listen to him more and more. What should they do? Should Puerto Rico break away from Spain? "No," said Baldorioty. "After studying the governments of the world, I think the best way is for Puerto Rico to be like Canada. Canada has not broken away from its mother country. It lives like a grown-up child, ruling itself, yet still paying respect to a wise and loving parent." This form of government he wanted is called autonomy.

This answer did not please the government, which did not want Puerto Rico to "grow up" at all. Nor did it please people who wanted to break completely with Spain. But enough citizens agreed with Baldorioty's ideas to elect him Deputy to the *Cortes* of 1869.

In Spain, he worked hard for the final abolition of slavery. He founded a publication, *Affairs of Puerto Rico*, to fight for that cause. He was largely responsible for the Moret Law, which made it a crime to be cruel to slaves or to sell children without their mothers.

Because of his Indian blood, Baldorioty's skin was a little darker than that of the Spaniards, though he was not black. One day a Deputy named Navarro Rodrigo saw him come into the *Cortes* and decided to make fun of his color. "The sky has clouded over," Rodrigo said.

Baldorioty looked out the window. "It's true," he said. "The sky is dark. But to understand something is to give light. Those who deny liberty to the slaves may have white skins, but their consciences are blacker than the skin of the Negro. My skin is dark, gentlemen Deputies, but here"—he pointed to his forehead—"here is light that comes out to brighten these darkened consciences." The Deputies stood up, clapping their hands for him.

Baldorioty's abilities much impressed the Spanish. The Minister of Finance, Laureano Figuerola, offered him an important job in the government. Baldorioty refused: "I can not serve a colonial government that it is my duty to oppose."

He was re-elected to the *Cortes* several times. In 1870, the *Cortes* was asked to approve of the naming of Amadeo de Saboya as King of Spain. Three Deputies refused to do so, casting blank ballots, instead of voting yes. One of them was Baldorioty, who said, "Never, not for anything nor anyone, can I betray my principles." For a colonial to act so firmly was asking for trouble.

It was typical of Baldorioty. A fellow member of the *Cortes*, the great Spanish orator, Francisco Pi y Margall, later called him "the great Deputy", and added, "He was a serious man, with a warm heart and firm beliefs. I never saw him hesitate to take a stand on a difficult question. Later, I saw him fight without resting in Puerto Rico for liberty. Persecution never discouraged him, nor did winning make him proud. He was as modest as he was brave."

He was generous, too. Going home after one meeting of the *Cortes*, he went to buy his ticket. At the steamship office, he met a poor writer and his wife, friends, who were going home, too. They had only enough money to buy the very cheapest tickets, which meant they would travel in the bottom of the ship, sleeping on wooden benches, without fresh air and with poor food.

Baldorioty himself had very little money. He bought a cheap ticket for himself and sent the rest of his money to the writer with a note that said, "You who travel with a lady need a decent and comfortable trip, but I can sleep anywhere. So please take this modest sum that I have left over, and have a happy journey." The writer tried to return the money, but he found that Baldorioty had already sailed.

Back in Puerto Rico, Baldorioty's opposition to the King came up to haunt him. He was elected Secretary of the Puerto Rican assembly, but the Governor refused to allow him to take the office. The Governor wrote to Spain, "A man who did not vote for the King who now rules the nation, a man who has boasted of casting a blank ballot, cannot serve here without at every step provoking conflicts. His political opinions have gained him a certain popularity among the poorer people. Some statements he has made put him on the side of men asking for liberty and reform."

Though he could not take the office, Baldorioty continued to fight. He argued for autonomy, demanded improvements in social and economic conditions and asked that more money be given to the *Sociedad Económica* for scholarships to educate young people. "We must educate our people if we want to be happy," he said. "Only through education can Puerto Rico end its enslavement as a colony."

For such statements, in March, 1871, the Governor ordered that he be fired from his job as a professor. It was his only source of income.

Three months later, in June, Baldorioty was again elected to the *Cortes*. But he was not re-elected in 1872. His own Liberal Party

Román Baldorioty de Castro in later life

betrayed him. The Governor at the time, Simon de la Torre, ordered the Liberals to support a man of his choice, General Fernando Fernández de Cordova, and some of the leaders obeyed the order. Baldorioty was not nominated.

Saddened, he moved to Rio Piedras. Life was going very badly for him. He was very poor and managed to live only because a friendly storekeeper gave him credit. He wrote to a friend in 1873, "The very bread my family eats hurts me. This blessed bread is an ever-growing debt to a friend's store, a friend who has little to feed his own children." Once he was invited to a feast. He would not go, explaining, "I cannot go to eat well when I know that my family will be eating badly."

He had many other troubles, too. A son died while still a boy. Two daughters, María and Matilda, died slowly of tuberculosis. His wife suffered from mental illness that grew steadily worse. He himself had much ill health.

Baldorioty returned to Ponce, where in April, 1873, he founded a newspaper called *The Right*. It lasted only six months. Then it was announced that an especially brutal former Governor, José Laureano Sanz, would return to Puerto Rico. Baldorioty found it wise to move to Santo Domingo where, with Arístides Díaz, he founded the Antillian College and taught navigation. He remained there for five years.

After his return to Puerto Rico in 1878, Ramón Marín Solá invited Baldorioty to take charge of his Ponce newspaper, *The Chronicle*. Baldorioty did so, and also taught part time at the Central College of Ponce. Though his health was poor and he seemed tired, he continued to fight for his ideals. In 1886, when he was nearly 65, the newspaper *El Pueblo* (The People) wrote, "His is a soul that does not grow old, a spirit that grows young again when his country needs him."

Baldorioty reorganized the Liberals into the Autonomist Party. Under his leadership they had a great meeting in a theatre called "The Pearl" in Ponce early in 1887. They demanded self-government, protection for individual rights, the right of every citizen to vote and many other reforms.

At the same time, something else new was happening in the island. All business, industry and agriculture were controlled by the Spaniards. There was only one bank, which loaned money at reasonable rates to the Spanish. But if a poor *jíbaro* wanted a loan, he not only had to pay very high interest, but also had to agree to sell his crop at whatever price the buyer asked. All good government jobs went to Spaniards.

Town mayors were appointed by the Government and were required to spy on the people. They were also usually rich merchants. Often they would not pay poor government workers or teachers, but instead would give such people "credit" at their stores. Teachers sometimes went unpaid for years in this way.

To fight such conditions, the Puerto Ricans formed a secret society called *La Torre del Viejo* (The Tower of the Old Man). Its aim was to help the people to own again at least some of their own country. Members of the group agreed that they would buy only from stores owned by Puerto Ricans. If there were no such store in a town, they would help a member to start one. Farmers would sell their crops only to members. All would band together to help sick people, widows and orphans.

In six months, the Tower had members all over the island. New businesses opened and old Puerto Rican ones suddenly prospered. The Spanish began to feel the pinch. They fought back, cutting off credit and supplies to Puerto Rican businesses. Some Spanish stores and warehouses were mysteriously set afire during the night.

The conservative people of the island, thoroughly frightened, asked Spain for help and a new Governor, Romualdo Palacio, was sent out. He decided to smash both the Tower and the self-government movement. He had a force called the *Guardia Civil*. (The words mean Civil Guards, but they were actually police.) He sent them out to arrest hundreds of people, who were thrown into jail without trial. Many were tortured. Such crimes were committed that the Puerto Ricans called 1887 *El Año Terrible* (The Year of Terror).

Baldorioty, Marín Solá and fourteen other leaders of the Autonomist Party were arrested in Ponce. One of the men arresting Baldorioty grabbed his arm. The old man shook him off fiercely, saying, "I'll go where you want me to, but don't touch me."

While he was in prison, Governor Palacio sent a messenger to see him. The Governor would set him free if he would sign a paper breaking up the Autonomist Party. Baldorioty replied, "I am a gentleman, and I cannot do such a thing. If the Governor wishes to kill me, he can do so, but I have lived as an honest man, and I will die an honest man."

He added, "When I leave this prison, if I leave, I will continue to preach autonomy. If the men are afraid to listen to me, I will preach it to the women."

One of his fellow prisoners was Francisco Cepeda Taborcías, an editor, who was Spanish. Cepeda said one day, "These *puertorriqueños* are behaving pretty badly towards us."

"You should be more grateful because this island helps you and has been good to you," Baldorioty replied.

"I know what I'm worth!"

"That's why I am so grateful," Baldorioty said. "I know how little I am worth."

The Governor ordered the prisoners to be brought by ship from Ponce to San Juan. There, they were to be locked up in *El Morro*—a great fortress overlooking the harbor—and then killed.

The prisoners were taken to *El Morro*, but before they could be murdered, Governor Palacio was recalled to Spain. They were freed on Christmas Eve, and never was there such a celebration!

Baldorioty's health was broken by the stay in prison. Soon after his release, he discovered that Cepeda and others were plotting to get rid of him as president of the Autonomist Party and take over control themselves.

El Morro — fortress and prison

Bitterly hurt, he resigned the presidency on January 2, 1889. "I don't know if I will ever again have the honorable misfortune to be in politics," he said. "I do not even wish to be named honorary president. I have been imprisoned both in military barracks and in the cellars of *El Morro*. What other honors do I need?"

A few months later, on September 30, he died. The Cuban patriot, José Martí, said of him, "Never in his life did he have it easy, the brave Baldorioty de Castro. He went to his grave poor, with his skinny hands upon his chest and on his forehead the immortal light."

Perhaps it is best to remember Baldorioty's own words: "Governments cannot kill the liberty to think. The idea, the thought, lives forever."

# CHAPTER V

## THE MAN WHO BOUGHT BABIES

A baby was to be baptized in the church, and on the steps outside a young doctor waited. Soon he saw what he was waiting for—a family of blacks, the mother carrying the baby in her arms.

The doctor hurried to speak to them before they could get to the church. They talked for a few moments. The doctor gave the mother some money. The family, weeping with joy, turned away from the church and left with the baby not baptized.

Dr. Betances had "bought" another baby.

A slave baby's freedom could be bought by paying 50 *pesos* to the owner if the child had been baptized. If he had not been baptized, the price was half as much—25 *pesos*. That is why the doctor used to wait outside the church to find unbaptized babies. The mother would take the money he gave her to the slaveowner and buy her child's freedom. The baby could always be baptized a little later, but he or she would grow up free!

What a difference that freedom made! Slaves in Puerto Rico were treated very cruelly. When the ships first brought them to the island from Africa, officers of the King's Army were waiting at the pier to collect a tax on each one. Lesser officials were also waiting and heating branding irons—like those used for cattle. After the tax was paid on a slave, the red-hot iron was pressed directly upon his body. With the smell of burning flesh and the screams of pain in the air, the slave was branded forever. If a slave were found without the brand mark, it was taken for granted that he had come to Puerto Rico without payment of the tax, and he could be taken from his master and sold.

*El Código Negro* (the Black Law) said, "Every person of the African race who fights against the whites, no matter how justified he may be, shall be shot to death, if he is a slave. If he is free, the executioner shall cut off his right hand, unless he has caused a wound, in which case he shall be shot." The law also stated that if any slave rebelled against his master, the owner could kill him.

No wonder that Dr. Betances wrote, "What a sad picture the trade in slaves presents on our island!"

The young man determined that he would spend his life fighting four causes: the abolition—or end—of slavery; the good health of people who needed his services as a doctor; independence for Puerto Rico, Cuba and Santo Domingo; and the combining of the three islands into a single Confederation of the Antilles (West Indies) to make one nation big and strong enough to earn the respect of the other nations of the world. Because of his work for this last dream, he was called *El Antillano* (The West Indian).

Ramón Emeterio Betances y Alarcón was born in Cabo Rojo on April 8, 1827, to well-off and respected parents. Even as a little boy he read books written for grown-ups. As a teenager, he talked openly of independence for Puerto Rico.

Unlike other boys, he was sent to France, not Spain, for his higher education. He studied first in the city of Toulouse and then went to the University in Paris to learn medicine.

Perhaps it was his French education that made Betances different from other Puerto Rican leaders. France had fought one bloody revolution for freedom. Now Paris was full of Frenchmen who were willing to fight again. Betances spent long evenings in the cafés talking and arguing with other young idealists who had noble aims. He heard the fiery speeches of the great French fighter for freedom, Victor Hugo. Soon, unlike other Puerto Ricans who believed that independence must be won peacefully, Betances came to think it could be won only through revolution.

In France Betances also began to make a reputation for himself both as a writer and as a brilliant man of medicine. He wrote poems, novels and plays which won much praise. He especially studied diseases which occur frequently in tropical countries like Puerto Rico, and began to have scientific articles published in

Paris, Madrid and Latin America. In 1853, at the age of 26, he finished his studies and went home.

He began to practice medicine in Mayagüez, but two years later one of the most awful events in the island's history took place—a dreadful outbreak of cholera, a terrible disease. It spread over almost the entire island, and before it ended, 30,000 people had died.

Dr. Ramon Emeterio Betances

For weeks Dr. Betances hardly slept at all. Because the disease was spread by filth, he issued regulations to improve sanitation. He was everywhere, taking care of all patients, not caring whether they could pay him. In one day he could wear out six fresh horses while he traveled to help the sick in distant places. Where the roads were good enough he rode in a little carriage, otherwise on horseback. Always there were healing medicines in the carriage or in his saddlebags, given free to the poor.

Dr. Betances became a national hero and was called *el Padre de los Pobres* (the Father of the Poor). In Mayagüez he started a hospital to which a school was later added. Even one of his enemies, a Spanish governor who wrote a report about Betances' revolutionary work, had to admit that "he does have all kind feelings and Christian charity which he demonstrates constantly, giving poor patients, not only his medical talents, but also all money he is able to afford".

Betances would not remain silent in the face of oppression. He spoke out constantly against the slave owners and the terrible conditions of the poor. The Governor ordered him to leave the country, and the doctor went back to Paris.

Before he left, he became engaged to a beautiful young girl, María del Carmen Henri, who was 19 years old and the daughter of his own sister, Clara. María del Carmen followed him to Paris where they were to be married. But just before the wedding, she caught typhoid fever and died on April 24, 1859.

A few months later, Puerto Rico changed Governors again, and it was safe for Betances to go home. He brought his sweetheart's body with him, to be buried permanently in her own lovely island. The coffin was in his own cabin on the ship for all of the long voyage across the ocean. He wrote a long story about her called *La Virgen de Borinquén* (The Virgin of Borinquén) and said in a letter to an uncle, "There are not enough tears to weep for her with."

Dr. Betances again took up the practice of medicine in Mayagüez and of course also went right back to his politics. With his friend, a young lawyer named Segundo Ruiz Belvis, he started a secret organization to work for freeing the slaves. On the mainland, the Civil War had begun in the United States, and the ideals of Abraham Lincoln inspired Betances and his friends.

In 1863, revolution broke out in Santo Domingo, and the Governor of Puerto Rico, Felix María de Messina Iglésias, sent two battalions of soldiers to help the Spanish government of Santo Domingo keep down the Dominican people. Betances saw this as a chance to strike a blow for Puerto Rican freedom. He wrote a message to the people which said:

"Puerto Ricans! For more than three centuries, Spanish tyranny has been oppressing us. Any sons of the island who have dared to say something for the good of their countrymen have been arrested, exiled and ruined.

"We have been paying heavy taxes, and we still don't have roads, railways, telegraphs or steamships.

"The worst people of Spain come to the island and, after squeezing the juice out of us, return to their land to enjoy millions that belong to us who did all the work.

"And now the government tries to make us hate our brothers in Santo Domingo, to make us go fight against them.

"Arise, Puerto Ricans! Let us show the dogs who rob and insult us that the *jíbaros* of Borinquén are not cowards! Let us unite against the oppressors of our land!"

Governor Messina was sure he knew who had written those words, and he called Betances to *la Fortaleza*. "If you continue this, I shall be obliged to hang you," the Governor warned.

Dr. Betances looked him straight in the eye. "General," he said coldly, "on that day's night, I will sleep better than you will."

Messina ordered Betances to leave the island, and for a short while he did so, but he soon returned after a new Governor had taken over.

However, he was not to stay at home long. In 1867, some soldiers rebelled against their officers. Betances and Ruiz Belvis were among those blamed for the rebellion, though they had nothing to do with it, and they were ordered to sail to Spain to be punished by the government there. Instead, the two friends fled by night in a small boat which put them ashore on Santo Domingo.

"The place where we landed is the worst land one can imagine," Betances wrote. "It is sandy along the shore, and inland it is full of barren rocks and populated by fierce mosquitoes. The heat was suffocating, the drinking water warm, the biscuits moldy and the cheese spoiled. I had a terrible fever and had to lie down, but the mosquitoes made me get up again to drink coffee. 'This coffee makes me think of our faraway land,' I said to Ruiz, and he smiled."

The friends went to New York where the story of their escape made a sensation in the newspapers. There they tried to enlist men and buy arms for the revolution. Ruiz went on a trip to Chile to seek help, and there, unhappily, he died. Betances then returned to Santo Domingo where he would be closer to Puerto Rico. From there it was easier for him to keep in touch with the members of the secret Revolutionary Committee who were still living in Puerto Rico.

The conspirators had to be very careful indeed, for spies watched everyone in Puerto Rico. The revolutionists were organized into little secret groups, with only the leaders knowing people in more than one group. They had a secret system for recognizing one another. When one of them shook hands with someone else, he would tap twice with his index finger very lightly on the other person's little finger—so lightly that it would not be noticed unless one were looking out for it. If the other person recognized the tap, he would say:

"What work do you do?"

"Useful work."

"Give me a letter."

"L."

"M," was the final answer.

The letters stood for *Libertad o Muerte*—Liberty or Death.

In Santo Domingo, in 1867, Betances married Simplícita Jiménez, who had been his servant since he lived in Mayagüez. He also managed to scrape up enough money to buy from the United States 500 rifles, six small cannon, some ammunition and a little ship called *El Telégrafo* (The Telegraph).

The government of Santo Domingo discovered that Betances was plotting, and the police nabbed him as he and some cousins of his were trying to climb a ladder to hide on the roof of the American Consulate. After they had been in jail a few days, the Minister of the Interior became very ill and wanted Dr. Betances to treat him. Betances refused to do so unless he and his cousins were freed. They were, and he cured the Minister.

Not long afterwards, the government came after him again. But Betances had declared his intention of becoming a citizen of the United States, and the American Consulate saved him. (He never followed through on that intention. Some years later he became a citizen of the Dominican Republic instead.)

As the date for the planned revolution drew near, the plotters back in Puerto Rico were in trouble, too. The group at the town of Camuy was betrayed and all were arrested. As a result, the entire coastline of the island was reinforced. Betances, who had been about to sail from Santo Domingo with men and arms on *El Telégrafo*, was blocked by the local government at the request of the Governor of Puerto Rico.

Because of the arrests at Camuy, the other revolutionaries on the island decided they had better move at once before they should all be betrayed. On September 23, 1868, they met near Lares at the ranch of Manual Rojes, who was leader of the group there. Among them were Mathias Bruckman, an American, leader of the Mayagüez group, and Pablo Rivera, who, although he was only sixteen years old, was named captain of the cavalry.

They had 400 men and a few horses. For the most part, their only arms were knives aand *machetes*—sharp-bladed tools that the *jíbaros* used for cutting sugar cane. They marched on Lares at midnight and took possession of it. Next morning they proclaimed the new Republic of Puerto Rico, named a provisional government and attended a solemn mass of victory in the local church. In other parts of the island, other groups were also supposed to be rising—but most of them never got the message.

The little army then set out to take San Sebastian where they hoped to seize stores of arms and ammunition. But there they met the Spanish soldiers. The ill-armed, ragged *jíbaros* could not stand against rifles, swords and cannon. The mini-battle at San Sebastian ended Puerto Rico's only armed rebellion.

The news of the defeat, and messages to those leaders who had remained behind to hold Lares, were carried by young Captain Rivera in a long and furiously galloping ride. Many Puerto Ricans think of that ride much as Americans think of another famous ride that took place during their own Revolution—especially since the name of Pablo Rivera could be translated into English as Paul Revere!

Some of the rebels escaped into the hills. Many were arrested, so many that the jails of Arecibo and Aguadilla could not hold them all. A disease that the prisoners called the "black vomit" broke out in the crowded prisons and killed 80 of them. The others were lucky. A new Republican government came to power in Spain at just the right time and pardoned them.

Betances was beaten for the time being, but he was not broken. If he could not revolutionize Puerto Rico at once, perhaps he could help promote revolution in the other parts of his dreamed-for Confederation of the Antilles—Cuba and Santo Domingo. When the Caribbean governments made things too hot for him, as they frequently did, he would move to New York for a while and work from there.

In 1872, a tired Dr. Betances moved to Paris where he devoted himself to medicine and to scientific research, though he did not forget the revolution. In 1875, he returned to the Caribbean for another attempt, but when it became clear that there would be no revolution in Puerto Rico, he went back to Paris again in 1878, this time to stay.

In Paris he was a brilliant success. His writings and speeches, as fine in French as in his own Spanish, made him famous. He was considered one of the best doctors and scientists in France, and treated even a former Queen of Spain successfully. He founded the Latin-American Hospital in Paris.

His kindness never left him. A friend, the writer Luis Bonafoux, was with him one day when a sick man who had come all the way from Spain to see the great doctor arrived. Dr. Betances gave the man a note that would get him into the hospital and said, "Now, my friend, we shall get you well."

"Oh, I hope so," the man said, "because I want to go to Cuba and fight the revolutionaries there."

He did not know that the doctor he was talking with was the official representative in Paris of the Cuban revolutionaries and spent much of his time raising money to help them!

Says Bonafoux, "A sad smile came across the kind Puerto Rican's lips. Then, collecting himself at once, he told the penniless patient, 'Here are 20 *francs* for a start. Afterwards, we shall see what else we can do for you'."

Dr. Betances, after he had taken Dominican citizenship, became that country's Minister in France. Asked to run for the Presidency of the Dominican Republic, he refused.

In 1893, Betances' health began to fail, and it continued to do so, slowly. When the United States declared war on Spain in 1898, he was an invalid. He lived to taste the bitterness of seeing a truce signed on August 12, placing his beloved island under the rule of another nation.

A month and four days later, on September 16, 1898, he died.

## CHAPTER VI

**THE EMANCIPATOR**

Near the town of Hormigueros the jungle growth almost hides an old ruined house. It used to be a large plantation's house—a hacienda—called the *Luisa Josefa*. Some country people believe that the ruins of such old plantations are haunted by the ghosts of unhappy slaves. But this ruin, at least, is not haunted. Nobody whipped slaves at the *Luisa Josefa*, or fed them dirty scraps or let them wear rags. Only the jungle animals haunt this ruin.

In 1829 the *Luisa Josefa* was a busy, happy place. The owner, Don José Antonio Ruiz Gandia, and his Venezuelan wife, Doña Manuela Belvis García, were happy because they lived with kindness. The house servants and the hundreds of slaves who worked the land were contented because they knew how lucky they were. They knew how badly slaves were treated on many other plantations. They knew about the whippings called *"boca abajos"* (face downs) because a slave was ordered to lie down first with his face in the ground. They knew that other slaves often were locked in tiny, hot cells day after day without seeing another living person. But Don Antonio did not allow chains or punishment cells or whips on his plantation, and Doña Manuela loved him for it.

When, on May 13, a new son was born to the couple, every man, woman and child on the *Luisa Josefa* rejoiced. Even tiny slave babies just learning to walk brought flowers gripped in their fists for "the new little master". The baby was baptized Segundo Ruiz Belvis, and his father gave out coins to everyone in sight outside the church, so that they would remember the day.

When little Segundo grew old enough to trot around and start getting into trouble, Don Antonio called a slave whom he liked particularly because of his sweet nature.

"You now belong to my son," he told the black man. "I want you to stay with him and look after him for the rest of your life."

The man looked at the busy little boy and smiled.

"Yes, master. I will look after him all my life."

From that day on, he stayed with the boy and served his needs well, year after year. Segundo became a schoolboy. He went to grammar school in Aguadilla. Then he was sent for his secondary education to Caracas, in Venezuela, where his mother had many relatives who could keep an eye on him. Segundo was graduated with high grades, and then it was time for him to go to Spain to study law. His parents could afford it. They had more than three hundred slaves working on the plantation and making it pay.

On the ship sailing from Venezuela to Spain, Segundo was happy to make friends with another Puerto Rican young man, two years older than himself, also on his way to study in Europe. He meant to be a doctor and his name was Ramón Emeterio Betances. The two young men soon found that they shared a great love for their native island. It was the start of a lifelong friendship. At first Betances thought that Ruiz Belvis did not seem serious enough. But later he changed his mind.

In Spain also, Ruiz Belvis met other young Puerto Ricans, such as Eugenio María de Hostos, Benito Polo, Ramón Nadal. He made friends easily. Everybody liked young Ruiz Belvis. His good manners matched his good looks, and he was kind and gentle like his parents.

In 1860, he returned to his parents, now a fullfledged lawyer. There was a great celebration on the *Luisa Josefa* when the young master came back.

Nothing had changed very much while Ruiz Belvis had been away. Plantation owners did not agree about how to treat their slaves. One of them gave only filthy shacks and the worst possible food to his workers. He claimed that slaves were not really persons, but something closer to animals, so why should they live and eat better than animals? Doña Manuela reminded him that the Church taught that every slave had a soul and was therefore a

Segundo Ruiz Belvis

person. The man did not care. Don Antonio tried reminding him that a weak, sickly slave did less work and brought a smaller price than a healthy one—sometimes this argument made slaveowners a little more careful. Young Ruiz Belvis listened to all this. It almost made him sick. He decided to talk with his father.

Don Antonio had been waiting for this talk. For some days he had noticed that Segundo had much on his mind, but he gave his son time to bring up the subject.

It was not a happy conversation.

"Father, it is a shame to keep slaves. I can't stand to see people enslaved, working without pay all of their lives, just because their skins are dark. They do not live like human beings."

Don Antonio was surprised and hurt. "Segundo, you know our slaves are not badly treated. Instead of filthy barracks, ours have clean quarters, built strongly against the weather. I try to give them the best food possible. I see to it that they have clothes to wear, instead of rags. I do not allow torture here, or beatings."

"I know, father. Our slaves are the best kept in all Puerto Rico, probably. But, father, we do not give them what is more important than food, or clothing, or kindness. We do not give them freedom."

Don Antonio shook his head. He did not know what to say. Perhaps he was thinking of a lantern's glow in the night, seen often at the *Luisa Josefa*, which meant that Doña Manuela was on her way with her basket of medicines again to help a sick slave.

"Father this is your plantation—yet I want you to know that if, some day, it comes to me and I hold these slaves' lives in my hands, as you do, I will give them their freedom, to have as I do my own."

Poor Don Antonio. This meant that the *Luisa Josefa*, which he and his wife had built up so lovingly for their children and their children's children to enjoy, would come to an end. Without slaves, it would become a ruin.

Long before he was able to free his own slaves, Ruiz Belvis worked in every way he could against slavery. He joined his friend Betances—now a famous doctor for his great work during the plague—in buying freedom for unbaptized slave babies, in writing against slave ownership, in promoting laws to block slavery, and in recruiting members for their secret abolitionist society.

Meanwhile, his law career continued. He became Justice of the Peace, then later, Attorney-General of the Municipality of Mayagüez. He distinguished himself in both posts. In 1864 the Governor of Puerto Rico, General José María Marchesi, presided over a session of the Mayagüez Assembly. Though it broke the law to do it, the Governor used some public money in an improper way. None of the councilors dared to correct the Governor except Ruiz Belvis, who stood up and said he was against illegally using money belonging to the community. Marchesi was greatly angered and he arbitrarily discharged Ruiz Belvis from his post. But the young lawyer's fame grew further in the town.

In 1866 Segundo Ruiz Belvis was elected, together with José Julien Acosta and Francisco Mariano Quiñones, as Commissioner to the Spanish government in Madrid.

José Julien Acosta

Ruiz Belvis gave a party to celebrate his election. He still lived at the *Luisa Josefa* and he invited his friends there. They made many speeches congratulating their host and wishing him a safe trip to Spain. They made many toasts. The wine glasses twinkled in the candlelight. Ruiz Belvis' greatest happiness was because he would be able finally to speak against slavery where it counted, before the Spanish government. But before he left, he said, he wanted to take care of a personal matter.

"There is a person who has been ever at my side since I was a young child, and whom I esteem as though he were one of my own. He has never wanted to leave me, and I know that on this memorable night he is joyful. But I wish it known that, although he has remained with me, this man is free. I wish it known now in case death should surprise me far away from the island."

The guests followed his gaze to a door where an aged black servant with silver hair stood watching the party. He looked surprised and shy. But Ruiz Belvis put an arm around him and brought him forward.

"I wish to state before you all that this dear man is free. He is as free as I am."

The man, weeping, tried to kneel and kiss his former owner's hand, but Ruiz Belvis would not let him. Instead the two men hugged each other, while their audience burst into applause. Many men there had tears in their eyes.

In Spain at last, Ruiz Belvis, Acosta and Quiñones, on April 10, 1867, presented the famous *Informe* (Report) asking for the

Francisco Mariano Quiñones

abolition of slavery. Many years later, Quiñones wrote in a newspaper article that although, of course, Hostos, Baldorioty, Betances, Acosta, himself and so many others had often talked about abolition, the credit for writing the *Informe* belonged to Segundo Ruiz Belvis. He had dictated it as though it lived in his brain, then later worked and worked to make it perfect. Freedom for all human beings was his burning wish.

The *Informe* amazed everyone who heard or read it. It told the sad history of slavery in the world and in Puerto Rico. It described the fears of the owners whose living depended on slave labor. It discussed the problems that slaves would meet once they were made free. But above all it said, "No more waiting—free mankind now, now, now. We will solve the problems afterwards. Because each hour that we wait while even one man is a slave, is a crime against humanity."

As the famous Spanish statesman, Emilio Castelar, pointed out, these Commissioners from Puerto Rico, and many of their backers, were men whose incomes depended on slaves, too. Yet they were fighting for abolition with all their might. They truly believed in justice, even when it would make them poor.

The *Informe* was like a seed which Ruiz Belvis had planted and which he did not live to see grow up. But Betances, Acosta and the others watched during the following years a beautiful tall tree grow from that seed. All of Puerto Rico's 29,182 slaves were freed forever on March 22, 1873.

The three Commissioners returned to the island. There Ruiz Belvis learned that Don Antonio was dead, and the *Luisa Josefa* was his. True to the word he had given many years earlier, he freed his slaves. At one stroke he turned himself from a rich man into a poor one.

Naturally, the Governor had this strange man watched more closely than ever. He caused Ruiz Belvis trouble at every chance he could. One day in Mayagüez, the military commander, a Colonel Balboa, was rude to Ruiz Belvis, who pulled him off his horse right in the street and gave him a beating. When the Governor afterwards found an excuse to exile a number of patriots, he made very sure Ruiz Belvis was on the list.

Ruiz Belvis escaped with Betances to Santo Domingo, then to New York. Then he went on alone to Chile, where death, as he had said, surprised him far away from his island. He died on November 3, 1867, after a brief illness.

A Chilean friend, Antonio Cruz, paid two *pesos* for a second-hand coffin for him and six *pesos* more so that the coffin might occupy a niche in the public cemetery for one year. Except for Cruz, the heir to the *Luisa Josefa* might have had no proper grave, even for that little while.

Those who knew Ruiz Belvis never forgot him. He was one of those people who leaves a sweet memory in everyone he touches. Many, many years later, Betances said, "Even now, whenever I see a crowd of young patriots, I think I still see Ruiz Belvis' face among them.

"He was dignity made man."

# CHAPTER VII

## THE MAN WHO NEVER GAVE UP

Ramón Marín Solá was born to teach. While still a child himself he taught younger children in Arecibo to read and write and do arithmetic. In his teens he taught older children in Cabo Rojo more advanced subjects. When he became a man he began to show teachers how to teach. Then, as an older man, he tried to teach men ideas by means of his newspapers. But ideas are dangerous, and the government kept closing his papers. Each time this happened, Marín opened a new one, because men had to be taught to think. When he went to jail—he taught the other prisoners!

He was a man who never gave up.

Ramón Marín was born in Arecibo on January 12, 1832. He first went to school in the Liceo de San Felipe, run by a Spanish priest named Don Mariano Vidal. When he was twelve, Ramón found time to teach the neighbors' littler children.

At eighteen, Ramón got a job as assistant teacher in a school in Cabo Rojo. There the government had handed the education of 70 students to a really bad teacher. One of these students was Salvador Brau, who later became a great poet and historian.

Another writer asked him how he had ever learned anything under that dreadful teacher. Brau answered, "Fortunately, to make up for the incompetence of that man, there came an assistant to our school in Cabo Rojo. A youth from Arecibo who did not have a title yet, or even a beard. Thanks to him the pupils in that school were able to learn more than how to count syllables on their fingers. We had absolutely no text books, so he taught us from his own mind. His way of teaching was so clear, and such was the liking between him and the students, that in two years, when Governor Norzagaray visited the school and put the students through hard tests, we did very well. We had gone past arithmetic to second-year algebra. And our knowledge of Spanish grammar was sound."

Marín got his title of *Maestro de Primera Clase* (Teacher First Class) when he was 24 years old. Then a group of fathers from the town of Yabucoa came to beg him to open a school there. They were desperate, watching their children's bright, lively minds going to waste with no one to teach them properly. Marín agreed to start a school in Yabucoa. He ran this school for several years. Sometimes he would ask his pupils' parents to pay him in slaves—then he would free the slaves.

In 1865, Governor Messina ordered the school closed. He transferred Ramón Marín to the town of Patillas, without giving him a chance to speak for himself. He accused Marín of having taught the Yabucoa pupils to mock their government by making a drawing of a donkey with a map of Spain for its head!

After the revolt at Lares, Marín was jailed along with many other liberals but he was released when political prisoners were pardoned by Spain.

Marín went to Ponce to take the tests for the post of professor in the *Escuela Superior* (High School). He won, with the highest marks of all. Yet Governor José Laureano Sanz ordered that another man be hired, although Marín had won the competition, because "Señor Marín is anti-Spanish". Marín tried many times to get that post he had won. Thirteen years later, when Sanz was back in Puerto Rico as Governor for the second time, Marín tried again and was refused again. Marín never gave up and thirty years after the examination he finally got the post.

Marín stayed in Ponce and opened the last school which he would found, *El Museo de la Juventad* (The Museum of Youth), which started in 1870. This school was always rated excellent. One of the subjects taught there was English. Among the pupils indebted to Marín were to be many well-known men, like Dr. Salvador Carbonell, whom he would meet again in jail one day.

The Republican Government fell in Spain, the king was returned to the throne, and Governor Sanz in Puerto Rico forbade the training of teachers and closed all private schools where they might find jobs. The time had come for Marín to enlarge his field of teaching.

Now he wanted to teach his fellow men through the printing press. This important machine had reached Puerto Rico very late, 367 years after its invention in Europe. A French emigrant named Delarue had brought the first, small printing press to the island. Knowing its importance, Governor Toribio Montes bought it from him and, in 1807, printed the first government paper, *La Gaceta Oficial* (The Official Gazette). Whoever had the printing press had the great power of ideas.

Ramón Marín

Marín founded *El Avisador* (The Announcer) in 1874. This was followed by *La Crónica* (The Chronicle) which he started up twice. Then came *El Pueblo* (The People). Then *El Popular* (The Popular). In 1890 it was *El Diario de Ponce* (The Ponce Daily). At last he founded his final newspaper, *El Noticiero* (The Newssheet), which ended in 1897. In a way, of course, these were all one newspaper. The names changed because the island government closed Marín down many times, but he always started again somewhere else under a new name.

However, one time he gave up a paper of his own accord.

Marín had a great admiration for Baldorioty de Castro who, like himself, believed that "soldiers cannot kill ideas". Baldorioty, too, was a great teacher. When he returned from years of exile in Santo Domingo, Marín offered him his own newspaper, *La Crónica*. The older man accepted this generous offer and in 1880 moved to Ponce where he began running the paper.

Baldorioty used *La Crónica* as Marín had hoped he would. The tired, aging patriot came back to life in writing editorials. He used the paper to shoot ideas throughout the island which soon woke up autonomists everywhere. He called together the forces of the Liberal Reformist Party. Marín read him with great interest and went on working on his new paper, *El Pueblo*.

Marín's papers were like stinging bees to the government. Whatever they were named, they kept printing the truth. If taxes were too high, if judges were unfair, if customs duties were unequal, if the Civil Guards acted badly, if roads remained unbuilt, if new laws were unjust, Marín's paper said so. No wonder the men who ran the island hated him, from the Governor—every Governor in turn—to the newest, stupidest Civil Guard.

Sometimes one of Marín's "stinging bees" flew as far as Spain itself across the sea. An editorial from *El Pueblo* in 1883 said: "We wish the Spanish citizen of Puerto Rico not to be held inferior to the Spanish citizen in Spain. Over there, the right to vote is given to those who can read and write, or else who pay a tax. Why, in our overseas province, is that tax three times as high for merchants and five times as high for landowners? Apparently, the Spaniards overseas are not quite as Spanish as the rest. No! It is not possible that some citizens should be more favored than others!"

Marín enjoyed his battles in his newspaper. He enjoyed his family and his beautiful island. In the summertime he would take his family to a favorite Puerto Rican summer resort called *Los Baños* (The Baths), in Coamo, where bathing in the mineral waters was supposed to be especially healthful. Los Baños boasted that its 30 rooms could hold 100 guests. Each of its fifteen baths had marble floors and blue tiled walls, and *two* faucets for changing the water temperature. Marín liked all this. Besides, at Los Baños he could always find someone to argue about ideas with him.

Back in the city, Marín added to the pleasures of life himself, writing poems and presenting plays. He wrote comedies with serious ideas in them that were presented in the theater *La Perla* (The Pearl). He was one of the founders of a literary society, the *Gabinete de Lectura Ponceño*. Named vice-director, he spoke at the opening dedication before the best of Ponce society in their finest clothes and jewels. This glittering evening was followed by many others which welcomed some of the greatest minds of that time.

But these pleasant times could not hide the fact that matters were growing worse and worse in the island's government. At last Marín felt he had to go to Spain and try to change things from there. If he could only get people to listen! He sailed to Spain in 1884. He stayed for two years, working all the time to improve the island's government. Some days he would believe he had gained help. Other days he would feel he was back where he started. Too many people had selfish interests.

Meanwhile, Puerto Rico was heading for *El Año Terrible*.

Marín returned home late in March, 1887, to find that the editor he had left in charge of his paper had been scared into printing opinions directly against his own. His own paper had been used to spread evil ideas!

In July, he and Baldorioty helped to welcome the new Governor, Don Romualdo Palacio, on his first official visit to Ponce. Judging that Ponce's mayor was too kindly to liberals, Palacio replaced him with his own nephew, Díez de Ulzurrum. Sadly, the citizens of Ponce said farewell to their previous mayor. Spies told Palacio that Marín's farewell speech had been highly dangerous.

The Civil Guards searched a house shared by three workingmen and found several dangerous publications, such as "Proclamation of War and Extermination of Spaniards". These were signed by initials, like the "A.M." used by Antonia Molina Vergara, a respectable old gentleman who was president of the Ponce Autonomist Committee, and the "R.M." used by Marín. The three workingmen were arrested, tied hand and foot, brutally whipped, then left for days in a filthy old warehouse infested by rats and snakes. Their arrest was useless; they could not swear who "A.M." and "R.M." and the others were, Governor Palacio wanted evidence he could show in court.

The Governor allowed the Civil Guards to get evidence any way they could. They sometimes used *palitos* (little sticks), wooden sticks covered with sharp nails and moved by straps, in which prisoners' hands and fingers could be squeezed. With evidence obtained this way, the Civil Guards arrested Baldorioty and Molina Vergara. The two elderly men were put in the Juana Díaz jail to wait for the judge.

However, the Governor had made one mistake; this judge was honest. Judge José García de Lara released the prisoners for lack of convincing evidence, and he released a lot of other prisoners as well. He criticized the great number of arrests.

A month later, the Governor had this judge replaced by another, also a José García, but a very different man, Judge José García de Paredes. In a few weeks, Molina Vergara was in jail once more. Newspapermen, like Ramón Marín Solá and Francisco Cepeda Taborcías, sometimes provided evidence in their own papers. Cepeda was arrested next. Furious, Marín wrote a famous editorial titled *"Hay País"* "There's a Country" in which he strongly criticized the Governor's actions.

Molina Vergara and other liberals in prison wrote Marín about what was happening to them. He printed the information. Soon, three Civil Guards arrived at the offices of *El Pueblo* and ordered Marín to take back what he had printed. Marín refused. The guards left, then returned and locked themselves in with Marín in the editor's office. Pointing a gun at his head, they forced him to sign an editorial taking back what he had said, and to print it in the very next edition of the paper.

Marín outsmarted them. He closed his own paper.

Governor Palacio was blocking all cable communication with Spain. The autonomists chose Marín and Baldorioty as the men who were to try to reach Spain by ship and tell the government about Palacio's reign of terror. The two friends had to apply to Mayor Ulzurrum for passports. Ulzurrum kept delaying. At last, on the very day they meant to sail, the mayor ran out of excuses and gave them passports. But he was cheating them. He sent word to Judge García de Paredes that two dangerous liberals were slipping out of his hands. The judge had long wanted to stop these two. He sent back an order of arrest. Marín and Baldorioty were about to board the ship when the guards arrested them.

The two friends were put in the local jail, then moved to Ponce's military barracks. Because the cells were full, they were locked in a store room. Upstairs, Molina Vergara and Cepeda Taborcías had been lucky—by being early arrivals they had been given a small, clean room. Most of the other prisoners could not even sleep because the cells were so tightly crowded with Palacio's victims. The prisoners wrote complaints about these conditions to Judge García de Paredes, but he did not answer them.

Another man trying to reach Spain by ship was arrested aboard the *Manuela* in San Juan. It was Dr. Salvador Carbonell, Marín's former pupil, who came to join him in jail.

A young pharmacist named Juan Arrillaga Roqué set out on the long, dusty road out of Ponce to try to succeed where older, experienced revolutionaries had failed. When he reached San Juan he secretly boarded a small ship headed, not towards Spain, but St. Thomas. There he transferred to a ship going to Europe. When he finally reached Spain young Arrillaga cabled back the code word *MUSICA* (MUSIC) meaning a safe arrival in Madrid.

Governor Palacio prepared to finish the troublemaking autonomists once and for all. He ordered Baldorioty, Marín, and fourteen other political prisoners to be sent to *el Morro* castle in San Juan. The Governor had a lady friend with whom he used to read Italian love stories. One evening he mentioned to her that when the Ponce prisoners arrived he planned to have them shot on the following day. The lady, who in spite of her bad taste in friends was a good patriot, told other people. Autonomists and decent people everywhere spread the terrible news. What could be done to stop Palacio?

The news reached Judge García de Paredes. He finally answered the prisoners' letters. He told them that when they reached *el Morro* all their troubles would be over.

The sixteen prisoners in Ponce were put aboard the warship *Fernando el Católico (Ferdinand the Catholic)* before dawn on November 8, 1887. They arrived just before midnight in San Juan, nearly all terribly seasick, and weakened further after their prison sufferings. Cepeda wrote, "We were hidden by a forest of bayonets. Marín could see little, he kept stumbling among the boards and rubble. Molina Vergara could no longer carry his bundles and we carried them for him."

At *el Morro*, a colonel, Don Francisco Cortes, called the roll, naming each man's title. When he reached the name of Epifanio Pressas, who was a humble shopkeeper, he did not even say 'mister'. He called the name twice more, but there was no answer. Finally, he asked directly, "Isn't that you?"

"I am *Don* Epifanio Pressas, although I am in disgrace."

The colonel looked into this brave man's face and said, "Pardon me, it was a mistake. Don Epifanio Pressas!"

"Present," replied the shopkeeper.

On the next day, the day set for the execution, the word *BANDERA* (FLAG) arrived from young Arrillaga in Madrid. This code word meant, "We have won all along the line!" (His two historic telegrams are today treasured in Ponce.) The Foreign Minister cabled Governor Palacio to relieve him of his post. The prisoners were saved.

Two days later, much against his will, Palacio handed over the rule of the island to his second-in-command, Juan Contreras Martínez, and sailed for Spain. He had been Governor for only seven months yet had left more wounds on the island that any other ruler.

Contreras was a sensible man. He did not believe the autonomists were as dangerous as Palacio had claimed. He ordered Judge García de Paredes to let the prisoners have visitors, especially their lawyers, and to start the paperwork for their release. The judge delayed as long as he dared but finally on Christmas Eve the sixteen prisoners of *el Morro* were set free.

Ponce prepared joyously to greet its returning heroes. A happy crowd walked around the ex-prisoners' carriages as they entered the town. Then, from around a corner came a group of Civil Guards, led by Díez de Ulzurrum, who blocked the way, hitting and slashing with their sabers, forcing the celebrants to scatter.

That same day, Baldorioty and Marín cabled Governor Contreras a request for justice. The telegram worked. The new Governor arrived in Ponce the following day. He had much to say to Ulzurrum. Soon afterwards, Palacio's nephew was removed from his post as mayor, and the extra groups of Civil Guards which had been placed in Ponce were sent back where they came from.

At the next election, when the conservatives claimed that Marín Solá could not run because he was still technically out on bail from *el Morro* and awaiting trial, Governor Contreras backed his nomination. Luis Muñoz Rivera, who was courting Marín's daughter Amalia, called Contreras "The only truly just Governor who ever set foot in *La Fortaleza*". Unfortunately, Contreras' replacement arrived in Puerto Rico on February 23, 1888. The long-suffering islanders had to wait and see once more what the new Governor would be like.

The next Governor, José Ruiz Dana, was a writer of sorts—he liked to write about the American Civil War—and when he first arrived he made friendly promises to the newspapermen. Marín was hopeful, but not for long. Conditions on the island soon grew bad again. The Civil Guard became rougher. When autonomists and other citizens complained to Governor Dana, he never answered. He earned the nickname *"La Silenciosa"* (The Silent One).

Paid gangsters roamed the streets, frightening liberals and doing the dirty work the authorities did not dare to do openly. Once, Marín was grabbed and beaten by one of these gangs. He went home and wrote furiously through the night. His editorials kept people from giving up.

He wrote until the end. He lived to see his son-in-law, Luis Muñoz Rivera, at last win autonomy from Spain, only to lose it again when the Americans conquered the island. He lived to meet his little grandson, Luis Muñoz Marín. His descendants would carry on the fight.

On September 13, 1902, there happened the only thing that ever made Ramón Marín Solá give up. That was the day he died.

CHAPTER **VIII**

**REVOLUTIONS ARE WON BY IDEAS—NOT BY HATRED**

On a poor farm at Río Cañas, a suburb of Mayagüez, lived Don Eugenio de Hostos and his beautiful wife, Doña María Hilaria de Bonilla. The night of January 10, 1839, was "sad, rainy and cold". Doña María was about to have a baby, but there was not even a comfortable bed for her. As she struggled with the pains of birth, her husband wept that she was forced to lie on a hard, wooden bunk. In the early hours of January 11, a son was born. They named him Eugenio María.

For two more years, the family tried to make a living on the farm, but it didn't work out. They moved into Mayagüez and then, in 1841, a terrible fire destroyed many houses and buildings in the city.

This tragedy that brought misfortune to so many people actually helped the Hostos family. Almost the whole city had to be rebuilt, but no one was allowed to nail two boards together or to place one brick on top of another without a permit from the Spanish authorities. As the young Hostos wrote later, "Under the Spanish colonial system, nothing can be done because everything requires the permission of the authorities. Slavery has as many shapes among us as there are things we need."

Don Eugenio was one of the few educated men in Mayagüez. His fellow citizens came to him by the hundreds to ask him to write their applications for permission to rebuild their houses. They paid him what they could, and even though he did much work without charge for those who could not pay, father Hostos' income increased. In time, he became an official, the Royal Notary, and he prospered.

Little Eugenio grew up in a big, two-story wooden house that was painted red and green. Like many big Spanish houses, it was built around a courtyard.

The house was full of people. Father Eugenio's offices were on the first floor and so was an apartment for Doña Maria's brother, Carlos, an elegant bachelor. Behind that were rooms for three black servants, headed by an old Biscayan gentleman named Adolfo. On the second floor lived little Eugenio; his parents; his three brothers, Pepe, Adolfo and Carlos; his two sisters, Engracia and Eladia; two unmarried ladies named Gumersinda and Escolástica; and more servants. With so many people around, there was always some excitement in that house!

A lot of it was made by little Eugenio, who used to pinch the maids and stick pins in the woman who did the laundry. He was considered a very emotional child.

A certain Doña Rafaela taught the neighborhood children reading, writing and prayers. One day Eugenio handed in a writing exercise that he thought was good work. To his hurt surprise, Doña Rafaela scolded him and punished him by making him kneel on the floor. He never forgot the incident and wrote years later that when he returned home, "probably never had a mother heard from a child's lips any more bitter complaints, any stronger protests, any more lively indignation" than he expressed that afternoon.

Hostos had had his first taste of injustice and he hated it from that moment on. "If you wish to know what justice is," he wrote later, "let injustice pursue you."

At the age of seven, Eugenio nearly died of an illness. It took him a very long time to get well again. Still he was a stubborn child. He wouldn't take his medicine unless he was bribed with a coin, and he kept the money in a little bag under his pillow.

From this terrible experience, too, he learned a lesson that he never forgot. He tells how his mother sat by his bed: "Beautiful, blonde woman, her face both kindly and impressive, sitting in the rocking chair, her sewing basket near her." When he could get out of bed, he would sit by her feet, cutting pictures out of paper and tugging at her skirt for a kiss. Little Eugenio was full of affection, and he learned to show that affection to people he loved, not to bottle it up inside him until it was too late. "Nearly all human beings love," he would write later, "but nearly none know how to love."

Eugenio especially loved his sister, Engracia. People often noticed the family resemblance between them, which did not please Eugenio because, he said, "I was ugly and she was beautiful". Sometimes as he walked to school or church, little girls would shout at him, *"Cabezón! Barrigón! "* ("Big head! Big belly! ") He said that truly he did have more than enough head for any man and more than enough belly for any boy.

Engracia was often bothered by a little dog in the house because it would nip at her ankles. One day she and Eugenio were on a balcony when the animal became especially annoying. In fright and anger, the girl picked it up and threw it down into the street. Badly hurt, the dog screamed and whimpered in pain. The children were shocked by what they had done and ran downstairs to help as well as they could. This was one more childhood lesson that Hostos never forgot. Never, in all the rest of his life, did he knowingly cause pain to a living thing.

Hostos went to school for a time in San Juan, but soon learned all there was to be learned there. When he was thirteen years old, his father sent him to Spain, where he studied at Bilbao and then, in 1857, entered the University at Madrid to study law. There was an epidemic of smallpox while he was there and Hostos caught the terrible disease while helping sick friends, but he recovered. Then, before graduation, he dropped out of law school to become a writer.

In 1862, his mother died, and Hostos wrote: "That event woke me from a dream of living. If there was ever a man who knows for sure what is real, and, above all, what a gap lies between real life and what adolescents imagine life to be, that man is myself. I learned that at the moment I lost the holy woman whom I admired as a living saint as much as I loved her warmly as a son."

In Spain he published his first book the following year when he was 24 years old. It was called *La Peregrinación de Bayoán (The Travels of Bayoán)*. It begins: "This book is more than a book. It is a wish; more than a wish, an intention; more than an intention, a thirst. It is the thirst for truth and justice."

The three main characters of the book represent the three big islands of the Antilles (West Indies), Cuba, Santo Domingo and Puerto Rico. It demanded freedom for them: "The Antilles will be for Spain if Spain gives them their rights, and against Spain if the era of domination continues." This was a very dangerous thing to say at the time, and Hostos was running the risk of prison. The book was not allowed to be sold in Puerto Rico.

Hostos was willing to take the risk. "There are complete men and incomplete men," he said. "If you would be a complete man, put all of your soul's strength into all of your life's actions."

Hostos joined a society for the abolition of slavery and continued to speak and write for freedom. There was a strong movement in Spain to get rid of Queen Isabella II and establish a republic. Hostos backed the republicans, hoping they would be willing to give Puerto Rico freedom. These hopes were dashed when one of their leaders told him, "Señor Hostos, I am a Spaniard first and a republican second," meaning that he was not willing to give Spain's colonies the rights he wanted for Spaniards themselves.

When students at the University rioted for freedom, Hostos joined them. As a result, he had to leave Madrid. He went to Barcelona and edited a newspaper there for a time. Then the republicans took power in Spain and introduced a new constitution which did not grant new rights to the colonies. Bitterly disappointed, Hostos said, "If in the constitution of Spain, there's no room for my country, then in Spain there's no room for me." He left the country, moved briefly to Paris and then, in 1869, went to New York, where Dr. Ramón Emeterio Betances and other Puerto Ricans were planning the revolution.

Hostos was poor. He had never made much money and never would, because he worked for his ideals, rather than for money.

When he arrived at New York, there was no one to meet him at the pier. And when he found his Puerto Rican compatriots, they gave him a cool reception. "As soon as we met, our friendship ended," Hostos wrote. "Their attitude seemed to be, 'Who had called me? What had I come for? What right had I to be there?' That was a terrible night. I felt more alone than ever before. They had no other reason than my poverty for receiving me in that manner."

Wherever he went, Hostos attracted beautiful young ladies. If he really had ever been ugly, he certainly was not now. He was of medium height, with a large, strong, masculine nose, a handsome beard and beautiful gray-green eyes. His good looks and his sweet, affectionate nature appealed to girls, and he responded the same way.

Hostos tells of a lovely daydream he had on New Year's Day, 1870, as he was walking along a New York street on his way back to where he was living. He imagines that he has gambled half a million *pesos* and won enough money to finance the revolution in Puerto Rico. He has also won the admiration of a beautiful young lady whose father is a very rich American. For his daughter's happiness, the rich man must help her future husband, so he supports the revolution.

Hostos plans the ideal revolution. There will not only be soldiers taking part; there will also be doctors, teachers, good people of all kinds. Hostos marries the girl and drills the workers in his father-in-law's factories. "President Grant, all the great American politicians, favor me. My agents are working in Colombia. Betances and the other leaders are boarding their ships to come to the island . . . .

"But just then I arrived at my front door. The revolution I had conceived remained where I always end up—in the shadows of desire."

Hostos found work in New York editing a newspaper for a group of Cuban revolutionaries, but after a while began to feel that he was not accomplishing much. In 1870, he decided to go to Peru.

He took a ship to what is now Panama, traveled across the isthmus and went to the office of a shipping company to buy a ticket to Peru. He had almost no money, so he asked for a third-class ticket. But he was well-dressed and his good manners impressed the ticket agent.

"The ticket is for you, sir? " the agent asked.

"For me."

"But gentlemen don't travel on deck, sir."

"Do men travel on deck?"

"Yes, sir. Blacks, servants, Indians."

"I am a man before I am a gentleman. I will travel on deck."

Hostos felt his poverty deeply. In Lima, Peru, he wrote in his diary on November 28, 1870: "What a thing it is to be poor and to live cheaply in a rich country where it's a kind of obligation to stay at the most expensive hotels! This has been making me feel a barrier between myself and many men. The more happily I spend an evening with intelligent, distinguished men, the more I dread the next day—for, when asked where I am staying, I answer the 'Hotel Seronvalle'. They ask one another, 'Where is that?' Then they admit they don't know the hotel, and they end up looking at me with inquisitive eyes."

Peru, like the western part of the United States, had imported men from China as cheap labor. Among other things, Hostos worked for the benefit of the Chinese laborers for a year.

One day a friend burst into his apartment and, in great excitement, dragged him off to the *Café Inglés*—the English Cafe—where he introduced Hostos to a rich Peruvian. The wealthy man owned a newspaper and needed an editor. He would give the job to Hostos and pay him 200 *pesos* a month, a very good salary indeed. Hostos thought it over, and refused. "How," he asked, "could I have come to Peru to free the Antilles and, instead, wind up in a fat job?"

But two days later, pinched for money, he wrote in his journal, "I could kick myself. I should have taken that job."

As he did almost everywhere, Hostos fell in love in Peru. He called her "Nolina". But by December, 1871, the time had come for him to leave for Chile to pursue his mission of finding help for those who were fighting for the freedom of the Antilles. It was hard for him to leave her. He wrote, "This is the highest price I have yet had to pay for my beliefs."

In Chile, he startled everybody by proposing that girls be taught science and other subjects that were then given only to boys. "By educating women to use all their brains," he said, "men will not only be just, but will also insure the future of a new social order in which women will apply their intelligence and warm feelings to the problems of living. Men are fools to entrust the upbringing of their sons, whom they expect to grow up to love freedom, to women who have never know freedom themselves."

Eugenio María de Hostos

He set out in the city of Valparaiso to find the grave of Ruiz Belvis. At the cemetary, he asked himself, "Where will I find him? Among the rich? No. Perhaps among the blacks, because he fought for their freedom all his life." But there was no grave there, either. When Ruiz was buried, his friends had been able to pay only a year's rent on the grave. The body had long since been thrown away.

"Then I thought that there is a little bit of him everywhere, because he loved all mankind," Hostos says. "And so, to all of those graves I said, 'Rest in peace, Segundo.'"

For the next few years, Hostos traveled a great deal, seldom staying long in one place. He went to Argentina, where he proposed the building of a railroad service across the mighty Andes mountains to the West Coast of South America. Then he went to New York where he edited a newspaper and was so poor that on many days he had no other food but fruit juice. From there, it was on to Santo Domingo, and then to Caracas, Venezuela, where in 1877 he married Belinda de Ayala, a lovely Cuban. He was 38 years old. She was fifteen.

Two days after his wedding, he wrote, "I wish these two days could last forever. Together we have celebrated the beauty of the sea, the splendor of the sky, the charms of being alone together. I pray silently that these days may go on. Happiness is absolutely new to me. Perhaps I should store some of it up to last me for the rest of my life."

In 1879, Hostos moved to Santo Domingo, where he was to stay for nine years. Almost single-handed, he raised the whole standard of education in that country. He founded schools and teachers' colleges and set far better standards of instruction.

He himself directed a school called the *Escuela Normal*. It was housed in what had been a convent and when the pupils were singing, Hostos would play for them on a small organ. One day a poor old woman passed, heard the singing and the organ and thought the school was still a convent. She came into the entrance hall and knelt to pray. Some students passed, and began to laugh and tease. In confusion, the old woman started to leave. Hostos saw what was happening and drew her back in. "Come back, señora," he said, "This is not a house without God. Here we shape the souls of citizens."

The fame of what Hostos was doing spread around Latin America and the government of Chile invited him there to improve their schools. He went in 1888. At the time, Chile had many teachers who had been trained in Germany and they were very strict, demanding absolute obedience from the children, which Hostos did not approve of. Though it made many teachers angry, he said that a teacher should be to his pupils like an understanding father.

Back in Puerto Rico, his own father was having hard times. Hostos wrote from Chile to Dr. Betances in 1892, "By reason of his old age and because he is the father of one who has exerted so much effort for his country, he should have the consideration of Puerto Ricans. Yet their conduct towards him is such that if the situation were changed in Puerto Rico, I would have to think very hard whether I would live there."

Hostos and his wife, whom he called "Inda", lived in Chile for almost ten years, and for once almost prosperously. They worked as a team; he would organize associations of teachers and then she would run them.

During his last days in that country, he had a disagreement with the Minister of Education and was called in to see the President of Chile. Hostos was, as usual, modestly, but very neatly, dressed. He maintained his point of view and looked straight at the President with his gray-green eyes. The President's eyes fell to Hostos' shoes, which were a little old-fashioned. He did not look up again. As Hostos was leaving, he said, "Sir, if I ever have to talk to the President of Chile again, I hope that he will talk more to Eugenio María de Hostos, and less to his shoes."

Then the United States declared war on Spain. Hostos told Inda they must leave at once for Puerto Rico, since his duty was to help his country. The poor wife, who had moved so often and so far, begged him not to break up the best home they had ever had. Hostos understood, but his hair grew whiter as his duty gnawed inside him. Inda saw his pain and gave in.

On the way, in Caracas, Hostos had to borrow money. On the note he signed, it says he meant to use the cash to "work for Puerto Rico's liberty."

Back in the island, Hostos organized the *Liga de Patriotas Puertorriqueños* (League of Puerto Rican Patriots). He had been back only a few weeks when a great assembly was held in the Municipal Theatre in San Juan to organize a delegation to Washington to try to persuade President McKinley to give the island freedom. Hostos was not a delegate to the convention, but he wanted to see what was happening, and took a seat in the audience.

Someone recognized him and interrupted the proceedings. "Do you know who that man is?" he asked the delegates. "That is Eugenio María de Hostos." The delegates rose to their feet, cheering and clapping and soon the whole crowd was shouting, "To Washington! To Washington!"

Hostos and three others were sent on the mission. They met in Washington with President McKinley and members of his Cabinet. Hostos spoke for the *puertorriqueños* seeking freedom. "The people of Puerto Rico do not ask favors," he said. "They demand justice." Afterwards, the Secretary of State described him as "that arrogant man from the tropics."

It did no good. The Puerto Ricans went home without having gained anything. Hostos set about trying to organize the people through his League of Patriots. He held meetings week after week, but found himself talking mostly to empty seats. The people were not about to fight. "I feel my country slipping through my fingers," he said.

After a year and a half of discouragement, he received a cable from the Dominican President: "Country, students calling you." He moved for the last time, and the Dominicans greeted him as though he were a savior, with parades, bands and flowered arches.

But soon there was a revolt in Santo Domingo. Hostos had the tragic experience of seeing his former pupils, on opposite sides, killing each other. At one point the lives of himself and his family were in danger and they had to take refuge aboard an American warship, *Atlanta*, until things calmed down.

In 1903, Hostos was 64 years old. He would come home from his work and sit in his garden overlooking the sea. There he would translate Latin classics into Spanish.

But one day he fell ill. Two of his doctors, former pupils, could not save him. On August 11, one of the doctors, looking out of the window, saw a storm approaching across the sea and mentioned it.

A weak voice came from the bed: "Lift me up, so that I can see." They raised Hostos in the bed and looking out at his beloved sea and at the terrible beauty of the approaching storm, he died.

Many of Hostos' sayings are famous in Puerto Rico. One of them is: "When you cannot be just because of your nature, be so through your pride."

Another: "Lend your light to the blind. Why should the wickedness of men irritate you, when it is only blindness?"

And another: "To be a *man* is the most extraordinary thing among the ordinary things of this earth."

Eugenio María de Hostos was a man.

# CHAPTER IX

## "WITH BROKEN WINGS, I WILL ARRIVE"

The soldiers rapped heavily on the front door, and Don Luis Muñoz Barrios opened it. "Your son organized a meeting and has been speaking against the government," a soldier said. "We have come to take him to jail."

"Wait a moment," Don Luis said. "I will get my hat and cane."

"Not you. We want the boy."

"My son is only 14 years old," Don Luis told them. "I am his father, and I am responsible for his actions. You will take me."

The soldiers did not know what to do. Muñoz Barrios was a leader of the Conservative Party. He was a well-to-do merchant and landowner and had been Mayor of the town. Could they arrest so important a person? The soldiers returned to headquarters for further instructions. They did not come back.

That was the first time that Luis Muñoz Rivera was saved from jail, but it was not to be the last. There were to be plenty of times when he would see a jail cell from the inside. Many years later, when he was once again on trial, the judge asked him if he had ever been arrested before. "Forty-two times, Your Honor," Muñoz Rivera said proudly, "and always for the same 'crime'—patriotism!"

Young Luis was the first child of Don Luis Muñoz Barrios and Doña Monserrate Rivera. He was born July 17, 1859, in the little town of Barranquitas, high in the mountains over Ponce. It was a sleepy village, with some streets so steep that even now an ordinary automobile cannot climb them. Later, when Muñoz was speaking at a meeting, people who opposed him would sing,

84

"Muñoz Rivera from Barranquitas eats *guayabas* and spits *pepitas*." *Guayabas* are a local fruit and *pepitas* are little seeds. The song meant that Muñoz was a "hill-billy", but nobody could hurt his feelings by calling him names like that.

As a boy, Luis soon learned all that the only school in town could teach him, so he continued to study with private teachers and by himself. He taught himself to read French. When his father happened to be going to San Juan and asked what present to bring back, the answer was always the same, "books!"

As a teen-ager, he took so much interest in politics that the Mayor—not his father at this time—wrote to the Governor saying, "We need more police here because in this district there is a very rebellious person." He meant Luis, of course.

The leaders of the local branch of the Liberal Party asked the "rebellious person" to speak at a meeting. Young Luis very much wanted to accept the offer, but he was deeply troubled. He told Don Luis of his worry: "You are a Conservative, father. I believe in the Liberal Party with all my heart, but I don't want to be disloyal to you."

Luis Muñoz Rivera as a young man

The elder Muñoz thought for a while. Then he said, "If you are loyal to what you believe in, you are loyal to me. Make the speech, my son."

Young Luis worked in the family store, Muñoz & Negrón, and became a partner, but his mind was on politics and poetry. He wanted to be a poet. One day the father showed the son a patriotic poem called *Adelante! (Forward!)* in the Ponce newspaper. "There!" the older man said. "There is a fine poem. Now if you could write something like that, then maybe you could think about being a poet."

Muñoz Rivera had written the poem and sent it into the newspaper under another name!

He wrote:

> I am going to the rough and unknown places;
> At the end, arriving with broken wings,
> But, at the end, I know I will arrive.

The day came when young Luis went down the mountainside to Ponce to meet Ramón Marín Solá, publisher of a fiercely honest newspaper. He also met Marín's daughter, the pretty Amalia. Admiring both the man and the girl, Muñoz Rivera was soon making the trip often.

In 1883, at the urging of Marín, Muñoz formally joined the Liberal Party, which stood for change and reform at Ponce. The party's leader who was the highly respected Román Baldorioty de Castro, liked him very much and introduced him to other leaders, saying, "I think he will carry on our work when we are gone."

In 1887, the Liberals voted to reorganize themselves into a new Autonomist Party, which would work for self-government like that enjoyed by the Canadian Dominion. The Spanish Governor, Romualdo Palacio, declared military law, and ordered the arrest of 400 Autonomist leaders, including Baldorioty and Marín Solá. Muñoz Rivera tells what happened in that Year of the Terror:

"The jails were full of citizens. The whip fell without stopping on the shoulders of the people. The special courts worked overtime—condemning, torturing, killing. Terror floated on the air."

Most newspaper editors did not dare report what was happening. One who did, Francesco Cepeda, of Ponce's *La Revista (The*

*Review)*, was arrested, beaten and locked up. A friend wrote Muñoz Rivera asking him to hurry to Ponce and take Cepeda's place to keep the paper going. He also warned that it would be dangerous.

"In the face of danger, worms dig themselves into the earth," Muñoz replied. "Men rise up and fight!" He went to Ponce at once. But he could not save the paper because the authorities made plain that if *The Review* appeared again, Cepeda would be killed in prison.

Word of what was happening at last got back to Spain, and Palacio was removed. But he had done his evil work. *El Año Terrible* broke the spirit of the Autonomists. Some members left the party, others quarreled among themselves and Baldorioty, now old and sick, resigned as leader. But some members carried on, and among them was "the rebellious person".

In 1889 there were elections for the Provincial Assembly, and Muñoz Rivera was chosen by the Autonomists to be their candidate in the district of Juana Díaz. Then the Conservatives picked Muñoz Barrios to be *their* candidate in the same district.

What a problem! Son just could not run against father! Out of respect for his father, Muñoz Rivera quit in Juana Díaz and ran in the district of Caguas instead. But out of respect for his beliefs, he spoke for the new Autonomist candidate in Juana Díaz, Manual Rossy. Rossy defeated Muñoz Barrios. Muñoz Rivera won in his district, too, but he never took his seat because the election was challenged by those who opposed him. By the time the courts decided that he had won fairly, the term of office was over.

In 1890, Muñoz Rivera decided to make a big change. He sold his share of Muñoz & Negrón and went down the mountain to Ponce to start a weekly newspaper. Ramón Marín helped him set up his little office. From the first issue of *La Democracia (Democracy)*, it was clear that a powerful new voice was to be heard. The paper was filled with reports of injustices to the people, and Muñoz Rivera's writing made the readers *feel*, as well as understand, what was happening. He was arrested many times, but nothing could stop him from printing the truth.

The paper gave new life to the Autonomist Party and to an old quarrel about the best way to get self-government. Muñoz Rivera argued that the best Puerto Rico could hope to win from Spain was autonomy—the right to handle her own problems in her own way while still remaining tied to the Mother Country. To expect Spain to give the island full independence, he said, was to ask the impossible. He wrote:

"Let us not dedicate ourselves to useless battles and the striving after goals impossible to attain. Let us follow the lighted star. Let us seek what is reasonable, not waste our courage on a struggle for dreams."

Muñoz did not spend all his time at the newspaper. Some of it was spent visiting Amalia or going to the Opera House where she sang small parts. In 1893, they were married.

Spain was under the rule of its Conservative Party headed by Antonio Cánovas de Castillo. Puerto Rico could expect nothing from Cánovas. So, Muñoz argued, why not make a deal with one of the Spanish opposition parties? Puerto Rico now had fourteen Deputies in the *Cortes*. Puerto Rico could offer the support of these Deputies to a party that would promise it autonomy.

He could not persuade many Autonomists. For one thing, Cánovas might stay in power for many years. For another, with

Práxedes Mateo Sagasta

which opposition party should they deal? Muñoz proposed the Liberal Fusion Party headed by Práxedes Mateo Sagasta.

A group headed by José Celso Barbosa strongly opposed any such deal, arguing that only a republican party would help Puerto Rico. But, Muñoz argued, the small Spanish Republican Party didn't stand a chance of coming to power, while the Liberals did.

For five years the quarrel went on, and Muñoz decided that the deadlock must be broken. He announced that he was ill and must travel for his health. He went to Spain, and once there, he was the liveliest "sick" man in the world. For five months he studied the political situation, attended meetings, talked to leaders.

He also found time to go to the theatre, the opera, the bullfights. He sent a steady stream of articles and editorials to his newspaper.

Then he came home. Now he was the man who had been there, who knew the Spanish leaders personally. Now he had the weapon he needed to convince his own party.

But first there was an unpleasant little business to take care of. On landing from the ship, Muñoz was met by an editor of *La Democracia* who told him that an article in the paper had offended Vincente Balbás Capó, a leading Conservative. Balbás had challenged "whoever is responsible" to a duel.

A cartoon showing Muñoz Rivera in court

Muñoz was outraged at the stupidity of such a thing. He wanted to say, "Pay no attention to the fool." But he was afraid that if he did so, his party would lose the respect of the many Puerto Ricans. So he said instead, "It's my paper. I'm responsible," and accepted the challenge.

Balbás was an experienced duellist, an expert with both sword and pistol. Muñoz had never held a sword in his hand nor fired a pistol at a human being in his life. He chose the sword, thinking that while he might be wounded, he had a better chance of not being killed.

For ten days he practiced with the sword. Barbosa—his political opponent, but his close personal friend—was his chief second.

When the day came, Muñoz tried desperately to defend himself. The skillful Balbás pressed in hard, and the point of his sword nicked Muñoz four times. He stepped back. "My honor is satisfied," he announced, and he walked away. As he passed his seconds, he said, "A brave man."

Afterwards, many people thought that Muñoz' pen might indeed have been mightier than Balbás's sword. Balbás might well have understood that to kill the editor of *La Democracia* would make him the most hated man in Puerto Rico and perhaps not sure of a long life for himself.

In 1896, Muñoz at last won his argument. He and three others were appointed as a commission to go to Spain on Puerto Rico's behalf. But when they got there, the top men were all busy, or out of town on holiday. The Puerto Ricans were told they must be patient. Three commissioners visited the government offices, listened to half-promises and were entertained by unimportant officials.

Not Muñoz. He got on a train, and he found Sagasta on a beach. The two men talked and Muñoz made his proposal: if Sagasta took over the government, the Puerto Rican Deputies would support his Liberal program, and he, in turn, would give the island autonomy.

"What if I turn you down?" Sagasta asked.

Muñoz knew he had one high card. Bloody revolution was going on in Cuba, and Spain wanted to keep her other colonies quiet. The Cuban Revolutionary Committee, operating in New York, had been urging the Puerto Ricans to join them.

Muñoz played his ace.

"I shall go home by way of New York."

Sagasta was silent for a long moment as the message soaked in. Then a smile broke over his face. "Don Luis," he said, "have an excellent cigar. And let us talk."

When the delegation sailed for home, Muñoz had an agreement in his pocket. The other commissioners had hands full of air.

The agreement was presented to a party meeting in February, 1897, and, after much bitter argument, it was approved. Barbosa led his followers out of the convention, and they formed the new Orthodox Autonomist Party. The Muñoz group became known again as the Liberal Party.

Muñoz had bet on the right horse. In August of the same year, Cánovas was murdered. Sagasta became Premier of Spain. In November, he kept his end of the bargain. The new Charter of Autonomy became effective November 25. A freely elected group of lawmakers would now make Puerto Rico's laws. The Spanish Governor's authority was reduced to almost nothing. Spain would control only foreign affairs, but the island would have a voice even in them.

Luis Muñoz Rivera as Resident Commissioner

A six-man Executive Council was at once formed to govern until elections could be held. Muñoz was given the most important post with the lovely title of Minister of Grace, Justice and Government. The word "Grace" was used to show that in this government mercy and justice would always go together.

He took office on February 8, 1898. Seven days later, the U.S. warship *Maine* was blown up in Havana harbor, setting off war between the United States and Spain.

Three days after that explosion, Doña Amalia presented Don Luis with a son. They named him José Luis Alberto Muñoz Marín.

The sadness of the event in Cuba overshadowed the joy of the one at home. "There the windows are broken," Muñoz Rivera said. "Here we will pay the bill."

General elections were held in March. The new body of lawmakers met on July 18 and named a new Executive Council with Muñoz at its head.

On July 25—just seven days after Puerto Rico's first freely elected government had come into existence—the United States invaded the island.

Under the command of General Nelson A. Miles, 3,415 soldiers landed at Guánica and began a march to San Juan, 70 miles away. There was little resistance. Most of the *puertorriqueños* greeted the invaders with smiles. Perhaps they would bring to the island some of the famous American riches and big business.

But the Americans took over the government and proclaimed military law. Puerto Rico's freedom—so new and so hard won—was gone.

Muñoz thought of Sisyphus, king of the ancient Greek city of Corinth. According to legend, Sisyphus offended the gods and was given a terrible punishment. He had to roll a great rock up the side of a mountain, but every time he got it near the top, the rock would slip away and roll back down to the bottom. Back down he must go to try again. but the same thing would happen, again and again for all time.

The heartbroken Muñoz wrote perhaps his most famous poem, *Sísifo*. His Sisyphus actually gets the rock to the mountain top. Then terrible lightning, thunder and "a wind from the north" shake the mountain and loosen the rock so that it falls again. This, he said, was the story of Puerto Rico and of his own life.

The Americans asked Muñoz to stay on to help them run the government. For a while he tried to do so, but he could not get along with General Guy V. Henry who was appointed Military Governor. Muñoz was a big and strong man, but on one occasion Henry said to the translator who was with them, "Tell Muñoz that I've knocked down bigger men than he."

Muñoz replied in a voice cold enough to freeze water, "Please inform the general that if he becomes violent with me I shall be obliged to throw him out of the window."

On December 19, 1898, Henry announced that he would permit elections only when he thought the Puerto Ricans were ready for such responsibility. The insult was too much for Muñoz. He and his cabinet resigned. Then Henry announced there would be no more cabinets. He and the men he appointed would run everything.

The Rock of Sisyphus had reached the bottom of the mountain.

Early in 1900, Muñoz started a new paper, *El Diario (the Journal)*, in San Juan. In April, the United States Congress passed the Foraker Act, a law which allowed Puerto Rico free trade with the United States, freedom from United States taxes, ended the military government and made the dollar, instead of the *peso*, the official money.

The Act provided for a civilian Governor to be appointed by Washington. The islanders could elect their own House of Representatives, but the Governor would appoint an Executive Council which could kill anything the House did. Washington or the Governor would also appoint all judges and department heads. Finally, the Act left the people with no citizenship at all. They were no longer citizens of Spain and not yet citizens of the United States. They were just "the people of Puerto Rico".

The *puertorriqueños* were divided about what to do. Some tried to join the American bussinessmen and get rich. Others began to fight for complete independence. Barbosa's group, renamed the Republican Party, took the side of the American authorities. A group of Socialists, led by Santiago Iglesias, tried to help the working people by organizing unions and leading strikes. The

Socialists were often arrested or beaten up. Muñoz did not agree with them, but he strongly defended their rights in his newspaper.

As the elections of 1900 came near, Muñoz's party—now calling themselves Federalists—feared they would be cheated. Many elections of the time were not honest. Votes cast for one side would not be counted, while the other side would fake many votes for itself, even listing dead people as having voted. The Federalists thought the election would be stolen in this way and—against the advice of Muñoz—told their supporters not to vote. As a result, the Republicans took almost every office.

In September, the Republican Mayor of San Juan, Manuel Egozcue, ordered the arrest of two Federalists and sentenced them to spend a month cleaning the streets of the city. When they refused to do so, he had them put into jail cells by themselves and fed them only bread and water.

Muñoz published a stinging editorial of protest in *El Diario*. Its title was *A Pack of Dogs on the Prowl*.

In tropical countries many people take a little nap—a *siesta*—after lunch. On the day that Muñoz's editorial appeared, September 14, while most of San Juan was enjoying the *siesta*, a gang broke into the offices and printshop of *El Diario* and wrecked much of the equipment.

But not all. The next day's paper appeared right on time. In it, word for word, was the same editorial, and this time it was printed right in the middle of page one. And the editor was at work in his office with a pistol in his desk drawer. For his courage, the people called him Don Luis *El Léon* (The Lion).

But during the night of September 18, about 100 men again broke into *El Diario*, and this time they destroyed it and then attacked Don Luis' home. With a few friends, and some shots fired into the air, he chased them off.

Muñoz moved his family to the safer town of Caguas, and there again started *La Democracia*. But all was not well. He was fighting his own people. His words in Puerto Rico were not being heard by the Americans on the mainland who were the only ones who had the power to change things. To talk to the Americans, he would have to go to their country. He resigned as leader of the Federalist

Party, put a good editor in charge of his newspaper and, early in 1901, took his wife and baby son to New York.

He started a paper called the *Puerto Rico Herald* on New York's West Side. It was published in English, which meant that his writings had to be translated. For the first issue he wrote an open letter to the President of the United States telling him how bad the Foraker Act was.

His paper did some good. In Puerto Rico, Santiago Iglesias was sentenced to more than three years in prison for breaking an old Spanish law that said it was a crime to try to bring about increases in wages. Muñoz wrote about the case in New York, and other American papers picked up the story. As a result, President Theodore Roosevelt himself ordered that Iglesias be set free and that Spanish law no longer be applied in the island.

In Puerto Rico, one of Muñoz's old friends, Rosendo Matienza Cintrón, was doing some thinking. Though he was a leader in the Republican Party, he came to believe that there could be no progress for the island as long as Puerto Ricans were fighting each other rather than the Americans. He wrote to Muñoz, proposing a union of his followers with the Federalists. The two groups joined into a new Unionist Party.

Muñoz went home to run for the House as a Unionist candidate. Back at his old desk at *La Democracia*, he was writing editorials that punched hard at the big sugar companies.

One day there was an unusual noise in the street outside. One of his workers locked the front door and ran into the editor's office. "Don Luis! Quick! Get out the back door!"

Muñoz looked out the window. He saw a crowd of perhaps 60 men. Some of the faces he had seen before. They were the gangsters who had wrecked *El Diario*.

"No," he said. "They are not going to ruin my paper again."

A voice called from the street, "Where is The Lion?"

And another, "Come out, Lion."

The front door opened. Out stepped a man, a big man, in shirt sleeves. He faced them squarely, tall and powerful.

"Here is your Lion!" he said in a voice that might have been a real lion's roar.

The crowd became silent.

"Well? " said the big man. "Who wants The Lion? "

He stepped forward. The nearest men stepped back. One by one, they turned away.

Muñoz went inside. "Everybody back to work," he said.

On election night in 1904, Muñoz sat on the balcony of his home in San Juan where messengers were arriving to report the results. A great crowd in the streets below cheered as each new piece of good news was called out.

A six-year-old boy watched everything in wide-eyed wonder. Luis Muñoz Marín has remembered that night all his life. The sight and sound of that crowd, calling his father's name, calling his father a hero! How did a man get to be a hero? And how happily they shouted, "We won! We won! "

But just winning was not enough. There was much work to do. In that same year, the American labor leader, Samuel Gompers, visited Puerto Rico, and reported:

"I have seen men working in the sugar mills 15 and 16 hours a day for 40 cents a day. I saw more men without work—not idle by choice, but because there was no work—than I have ever seen in my life. I have never seen so many women and children with the marks of hunger in their faces. No, never have I seen so much misery in one people."

These were the conditions that Muñoz hammered at in his editorials and in his speeches in the House. The House appointed him head of a committee of three to ask President William Howard Taft to improve the Foraker Act. "Taft roared like a lion wounded by the hunter's arrow," Muñoz reported. He turned down the request.

The Unionists won a smashing victory in the elections of 1910, and Muñoz was chosen to be Resident Commissioner in Washington. The Commissioner was Puerto Rico's representative in the United States. He was permitted to sit in the United States House of Representatives and to speak there, but he could not vote.

Don Luis knew he could not speak to Congress in Spanish. He would have to learn English. Besides, he was alone. He and Doña Amalia had not been getting along for some time, and now they were separated. She was living in New York. Young Luis was living away at school.

Muñoz sat down by himself in a room in the Willard Hotel in Washington to learn English at the age of 51. It was the loneliest year of his life.

As his ability with the language grew, he talked more and more to Congressmen, seeking their support, explaining Puerto Rico's problems. They learned to respect him for his honesty and his command of facts.

In 1913, new hope dawned. Woodrow Wilson became President, and in his first message to Congress he asked for "generous justice" for Puerto Rico and "full rights and privileges" for its people.

Don Luis moved into his last great battle. Inside his body, a slow and awful disease—cancer—was at work.

Congressman William A. Jones of Virginia introduced a bill to improve Puerto Rico's condition. It offered far less than Muñoz wanted, neither independence nor full self-government. Talks with President Wilson and Congressional leaders made plain to Muñoz that he could not have what he wanted. The best he could hope to do was to improve the Jones bill.

It was not easy. How do you interest a Congressman from, say, St. Louis, Missouri, or Great Falls, Montana, in the problem of a small faraway island when he has hardly even heard of the place at all? Muñoz did it.

As the bill was finally shaped, it replaced the appointed Executive Council with an elected Senate. It gave the vote to every adult male. It gave Puerto Ricans United States citizenship and a Bill of Rights, a promise that certain freedoms could not be taken away from anyone. The Governor, the judges of the Supreme Court and some department heads would still be appointed from Washington. The Governor could still kill acts of the legislature, but the legislature could appeal over his head to the President.

This certainly did not add up to independence, but it *was* a great improvement over the Foraker Act. When the bill came to a final vote in the House, Muñoz Rivera rose to speak. His talk had all of his old power and beauty of language, and it was delivered in perfect English. The House passed the bill on May 15, 1916.

Muñoz remained in Washington a few months more to make sure the Senate would also pass the bill, as it was expected to do early the following year. Then, tired and sick, he went home in September. Back in his beloved mountains of Barranquitas, his health failed steadily. He went to San Juan for treatment.

One evening, a friend at his bedside said to him, "Don Luis, the people of Puerto Rico are all with you."

"Then," Don Luis replied, "this is a good time to die."

Early the next morning, on November 15, 1916, The Lion went "to the silence and to his rest".

The Jones bill became law on March 2, 1917.

The Rock of Sisyphus passed to the hands of a boy who was then 18 years old.

# CHAPTER X

## "BLACK! BLACK! BLACK! I AM PROUD OF BEING NEGRO!"

Lucía Alcalá was always interested in education, though she never had much of it herself. She and her sister, Carmen, were the children of a Venezuelan couple. Their father had gotten into trouble with the government of that country and had to send his family away to Puerto Rico for safety. They never heard from him again, and when Carmen was two and Lucía was ten, their mother died.

Alone in the world, little Lucía had to look out both for herself and for Baby Carmen. Hungry and ragged, they lived for a time in the streets of San Juan. Then a kind lady, Señora Carmen Vega, took the two little black girls into her house, where Lucía worked hard as a servant so her sister could go to the school of Celestina Cordero.

Lucía fell ill one day, and Señora Vega sent her to recover at the home of a laundress in Bayamón. There she met a young man named Juan Tirado, who made cigars and had a little tobacco shop in the town. Soon they were married and Carmen came to live with them. Juan had a nephew, Hermógenes Barbosa, a house builder who specialized in chimneys. He did his work so well that he was called "King of the Chimneys". In spite of his good work, however, he was too poor to have a house of his own. When he married Carmen, he came to live with her at the house of his Uncle Juan and Lucía.

The Tirados had no children of their own, and were wildly happy on July 27, 1857, when Carmen gave birth to a son who was named José Celso.

Though Lucía was only eight years older than Carmen, she had been taking care of her for so long that she was as much mother as sister. In fact, the whole family called her Mamá Lucía. And for Pepito—"Little Joe"—she had one dream: he was going to become an educated man. To help pay for his education, she kept a few cows just outside of Bayamón. Besides taking care of her house, she would milk the cows every day, sell most of the milk and carefully put the money away.

When the little boy was four years old, Juan Tirado died. After her tears had dried, Mamá Lucía did some hard thinking. Hermógenes did not earn enough to keep the family going. She must make more money. She sold the cows and Tirado's tobacco shop and used the money to buy some small houses that she could rent. She was an expert with a needle and thread, and began to do sewing for some of the Bayamón ladies. And she was an excellent cook, so she made candy and pastries for stores in San Juan. Sometimes she would cook whole meals for neighbors to take out.

Little José was sent to a school run by Don Gabriel Ferrer Hernández. He loved Don Gabriel and worked very hard at his studies. When he was graduated at the age of twelve, he had won two medals, one for good work and the other for good conduct.

The school was poor, so the medals were to be of bronze. Mamá Lucía thought they should be of silver. She went to Don Gabriel and, with his permission, she paid extra to have them made of silver. How they shone when they were presented to young José!

Don Gabriel told José that he was leaving Bayamón. He had been teaching in order to save money so that he could go to Spain and study to become a doctor. José thought what a marvelous thing it must be to be a doctor, especially if so good a man as Don Gabriel would give up an excellent position as a teacher for it. Could he himself become a doctor? No, for a poor, black boy that must be impossible.

Could he even go on to the Seminary in San Juan, the only high school in Puerto Rico? Mamá Lucía was determined that he should.

"But we don't have the money," Hermógenes pointed out.

"I will work," said Mamá Lucía.

"But they won't take a black child,"

"They took Baldorioty and his mother was Indian."

She went to see the head of the school. She showed him the silver medals. She reminded him that she had done many things for the church, which operated the school. She was a very determined woman and José was admitted.

He could not live alone in San Juan, so Mamá Lucía moved there to make a home for him. He was very lonely at school being the only black child there and very poor. The wealthier boys of old Spanish families avoided him. His teachers did little to encourage him. Mamá Lucía arranged for him to take flute and violin lessons so that he would have something to do after school.

One day a teacher asked him in class what work he planned to do. Barbosa said he wanted to become a lawyer, a *licenciado*. The teacher said, "What you'll be is a *licenciado de presidio*"—a criminal who has been let out of jail. The students laughed. Barbosa never forgot that teacher's cruel remark. Years later, when he was a doctor, he reminded the man of it. The teacher said he had just been joking, that he had said it only to challenge Barbosa to work harder.

He *was* working hard. He thought he had won a medal in history, but the teacher gave it to someone else. Barbosa asked why, but the teacher's answer was not convincing. "I suppose there are differences even in Heaven, Father," the boy said bitterly. "What a surprise you'll get when you get there and find you're not sitting next to the Pope." He could have been expelled for talking like that, but he wasn't. Mamá Lucía consoled him, saying it was what he had learned that counts. "Nobody can take that away from you."

In his loneliness, young Barbosa took long walks through the streets of San Juan. He walked not only along the main avenues and through the public squares, but also the narrow, smelly little streets where the poorest people lived. What he saw made him determined that Puerto Rico must have a better life.

On some of his walks he would pass a place where he knew he would see a certain group of children playing. One of them, he thought, was the prettiest girl he had ever seen. Her playmates called her Belén. He was too shy to speak to her and did not even learn her last name, but he never forgot her.

At the age of eighteen, Barbosa was graduated from the Seminary and returned to Bayamón, where his father was working as a foreman on a sugar plantation. The planter, Don José Escolástico Berriós, hired the son, too, to teach his three little boys. He soon grew to like the young man and offered to help him continue his education. Don José brought Barbosa a ticket to New York and gave him introductions to friends there. Before he left, Barbosa learned as much English as he could from an English lady who tutored Don José's daughters.

Dr. José Celso Barbosa

He went to a private school in New York to improve his English. Though most of the students were white, he made many friends. Among them were two girls, first a German, then an American, both rich and both white. They wanted to marry him, but Barbosa said, "I'll never marry a woman who could throw up to me either my color or her money!"

Another friend was a doctor, who encouraged him to study medicine. What was impossible in Puerto Rico could be done in the United States. In 1877, Barbosa entered the medical school of the University of Michigan at Ann Arbor. There his excellent work and warm personality won him the respect and affection of his classmates. He was graduated in 1880, spent a few months of further study in American hospitals and went home to Puerto Rico.

Trouble again. The authorities would not give him a license to practice medicine. They said it was because he had not studied at a European medical school and that the University of Michigan was not good enough. Barbosa went to see the American Consul, who represented the United States government in San Juan. The Consul went to see the Governor, telling him that the University of Michigan had a very good medical school indeed. Barbosa got his license.

He soon had a very busy practice. His waiting room was always packed with poor people, whom he treated for whatever they could pay, or for nothing at all. Often the doctor would "pay" the patient. He would slip a prescription into a poor man's hand. Folded inside it would be the money to buy the drugs the man needed. But Barbosa also had enough patients who could pay, and he prospered. He brought his family from Bayamón to live with him in San Juan.

Dr. Barbosa also took some interest in politics. Once, giving a speech in Aguadilla, he compared the republican form of government to monarchy. A man interrupted him, saying that the military commander of the district wanted him to change the subject. Dr. Barbosa went right on. The man interrupted again. "Tell your chief," the doctor said, "that I will be happy to duel with him whenever he pleases." Barbosa was known to be an expert swordsman. He was not interrupted again.

Once the doctor was called to see a young woman who had laryngitis, a sickness of the throat that makes the patient talk in a hoarse whisper. Barbosa examined her, prescribed treatment and said he would call again the next day.

After he had left the house, a thought struck him. She looked very much like the little girl, Belén, whom he had admired years before. Was she? He knew only that she was a Miss Sanchez. He didn't know her first name.

The possibility bothered him all night. Early next morning, entering her room, he took a chance: "Good morning, Belén. How are you?"

"Better, thank you, doctor," she whispered.

It was she! For years afterwards, Barbosa would tease her by imitating the way she had whispered at him when she had laryngitis.

They were married on June 9, 1885. After the wedding, Mamá Lucía offered the household keys to the bride, who refused them. She asked Mamá to remain mistress of the household. Mamá did so, but not for very long. She died in 1888 and Carmen died only a year later.

Barbosa and Belén were a happy couple in spite of the fact that she had left school at the age of eight. She loved books, however, and had read a great deal more than most young women.

For some years Barbosa was not active in politics, though he believed that Puerto Rico should have autonomy so that it could set up its own republican government. Then a leader of the Conservative Party said to him, "Doctor, we like fellows like you who don't go around attacking the government." That made Barbosa so mad that he joined the Liberal Party the next day.

When Baldorioty called the big conference of the Liberals at Ponce in 1887 to organize the Autonomist Party, Barbosa was a delegate from San Juan. He also joined the Society of the Old Man's Tower. But in spite of his leadership in the party, he was not one of those arrested in the round-up of *el Año Terrible*. He had too many patients who were important Conservatives and who would complain if they lost their family doctor.

Thus Barbosa was spared the horrors his friends underwent in *el Morro*, but he was able to do one thing for them. On the night before the executions were to take place, a friend of his learned that Governor Palacio had been recalled to Spain and ran all the way to Barbosa's house to tell him.

How to get the good news to the prisoners? When *el Morro* opened for business at eight o'clock the next morning, Dr. Barbosa was waiting at the gate. "The wife of the military governor of *el Morro* called for me," he said. "She is ill. Take me to her apartment."

A guard led him through the prison and, on the way, could not resist boasting, "There's where we put the prisoners from Ponce." Barbosa ran toward the cells and hit the jackpot! Looking at him through the bars was Baldorioty himself! "The Governor has been recalled!" the doctor shouted. The guard pulled him away, scolding, but the good news had been delivered.

After *el Año Terrible*, Barbosa was one of those who stayed with Muñoz Rivera and worked to rebuild the Autonomist Party. He also continued to practice medicine.

One day he was called to the house of a rich man who was very ill. Dr. Barbosa had to tell the man's wife that there was nothing he could do. Her husband was dying.

The unhappy woman called in another doctor. This man told her that with a series of expensive treatments he could save her husband. When Dr. Barbosa returned, the wife told him the glad "news".

Barbosa knew the other doctor. He told the woman to stand behind a screen and listen to them talk. Then he told the other doctor he thought the man was dying and could not be saved. "Sure, you're right," the other doctor said. "But these people have got money. Let's get some of it while we can."

Dr. Barbosa drew aside the screen. Furious, the crooked doctor left.

He wanted revenge and he tried to get it. A few months later, in 1890, Barbosa was invited to become a professor at the Puerto Rico Atheneum, but first he had to take an examination to prove that he knew enough to teach medical subjects, even though he was one of the best known doctors on the island.

Just before the examination, the crooked doctor gave a dinner for the group of doctors who had come from Cuba especially to question Barbosa. He told them many lies about Barbosa, and they left his house despising a man they had never met.

At the examination, the doctors treated Barbosa unbelievably badly. One of them refused to wear his official robes to examine a colored man. All of them were rude, arrogant and tried to make things as hard for Barbosa as possible. Some of Barbosa's friends who were present were so angry at the way he was being treated, they walked out. Later, Barbosa was to say that the two days of the examination were the worst of his life. Yet he did so well that at the end the president of the examining board congratulated him.

At this time, the dispute was beginning within the Autonomist Party over the best way to win Puerto Rico's freedom. The quarrel came to a head when Muñoz Rivera obtained the Sagasta Agreement. Barbosa could not accept it, believing that the autonomy it granted was false because Puerto Rico still could not have a republic. "Muñoz," he said, "I have autonomy here"—he slapped his forehead—"but I have my country *here*"—and he tapped his heart. He and his followers withdrew from the party of Muñoz and became known as *puros*.

Though the two men were bitter opponents politically, they kept a friendship and respect for each other, as two exactly opposite stories show. One time when Barbosa was campaigning, a woman who favored Muñoz shouted at him, "Muera Barbosa! " ("Death to Barbosa! "). His reply was, "Viva Muñoz! " ("Long live Muñoz! ").

And Luis Muñoz Marín said that his earliest memory of Barbosa was being taught by some grown-ups to say, "Muera Barbosa! " and then being sent to say it in front of his father, who was writing. Muñoz Rivera dropped his pen and lifted the boy atop the desk. "Who taught you that? " he demanded. "I will not let you down until you say, 'Viva Barbosa! ' instead." Close to tears, the little boy did as he was told. His father warned him, "Don't let me hear you say 'muera' again."

Dr. Barbosa was in Bayamón on May 12, 1898, when he heard the thunder of eight United States warships opening fire on San Juan. With him was another doctor, Gabriel Ferrer—his old teacher—and two other men. Because people might be wounded and need the doctors' help, the four started at once for San Juan.

To get all the way by land would take hours. Instead, they went by carriage to the town of Catano, across the harbor from San Juan. There they convinced the crew of a small boat to take them over the water. The bombardment was going on. Shells struck in the bay around them, some so close that those in the boat were actually splashed. They reached land safely, and the doctors hurried off to the hospital.

Ever since he had studied at Michigan, Barbosa had felt friendly towards the United States. When Puerto Rico became an American possession, he hoped that the island would become "a territory today and a State of the Union tomorrow", His *puros* changed their name to the Republican Party and Barbosa tried to work with the Americans.

The Foraker Act established an Executive Council as the upper house of the legislative assembly. The eleven members were all appointed by the President of the United States and only five of them could be Puerto Ricans. Barbosa was one of the five, and thus held one of the highest offices a Puerto Rican could.

The new assembly passed some good laws. Barbosa worked especially hard for a Bill of Rights, like that of the United States Constitution, and for a law giving scholarships to poor Puerto Ricans who wanted to study at United States colleges. He was the only member of the Executive Council to be appointed five times in a row and he remained a member until 1917 when the Jones Act abolished the Council.

Barbosa was elected to the new Senate in 1917 and again in 1920. He continued to work to try to better conditions for the poor. "One cannot say one controls a country if one does not control its wealth," he wrote. "Puerto Ricans! Work constantly with one purpose only—to recover our lands and to be the owners of our country."

Barbosa was the real leader of the Republican Party, but he refused to be called that, partly because he thought that some people might vote against the party if its leader were a black man. "Black! Black! Black! " he wrote. "I am proud of being Negro. Nor have I ever tried to beg tolerance from anyone. Superiority is not proved by color, but by the brain, by education, by will power, by moral courage."

Another reason why he would not take the official leadership was his modesty. In his last years, he refused to have his picture taken and he was greatly upset when some friends wanted him to pose for a bronze statue of his head. It would not be right, he said, because the work that the statue was to honor "was not Barbosa's doing, but the doings of a group of men with high, noble and generous ideas. That work was a collective work."

Nevertheless, he was at last persuaded to pose for the sculptor, Marcos Coll. Barbosa was ill with a cancer that was soon to kill him, and he knew it. He found it very tiring to pose, and told the artist, "Ah, friend Coll, now I understand how well models earn their pay."

Perhaps Barbosa's modesty also helped to explain his love of cigars, because his face was almost always half hidden in a cloud of blue smoke. In the evenings he would sit in the living room of his house at Number 28 Salvador Brau, facing the Plaza Baldorioty, smoking, while his daughter, Carmen Belén, played the piano for him.

Outside, not a vacant seat could be found on the benches in the little plaza, as people gathered to hear the music coming through the open windows. Clerks from the corner drugstore would not go home when it closed at ten o'clock, but would stand in the street listening. Even the men in the neighborhood billiard room would stop playing their games. Those who looked into the half-dark living room could see the glow of the doctor's cigar tip as he listened, surrounded by those of his nine sons and daughters who were at home. And when at last the people outside would hear Carmen Belén play her father's favorite piece, A.S. Sweet's *La Madonna*, they knew the concert was over, and it was time to say good-night.

By 1921, his family, too, knew that he had cancer. One son, Manolo, wanted to put off his departure for the United States, where he was to go to college. "Go on, son," Dr. Barbosa urged. "Don't waste your time here." Manolo went.

In September his doctors—including another son, Guillermo—told him they would have to operate. "All right," said Dr. Barbosa, "but do it here. I want to die at home."

"But, Papa, we can't do it here," said Guillermo, "There's too much breeze for us to use the anesthetic."

"You can close the windows," said the old man. "I was a surgeon before you, and I know what can be done."

Another doctor spoke. "Dr. Barbosa," he said, "we are responsible for your treatment. You cannot ask us to work under poor conditions." Barbosa gave in.

The operation was performed on September 15, but it did not help.

On September 21, just before he died, Dr. Barbosa said, "There is nothing I would change. If I had my life to live over, I would live it the same way."

The family sent a cablegram to Manolo in New York: "Papa is resting."

CHAPTER XI

**RISE UP! REVOLT! RESIST!**

The courtroom was in Puerto Rico, but one of the lawyers was from the United States—Kentucky to be exact. He was the prosecutor, the lawyer whose job it is to present the evidence against people accused of crime. He was talking to the jury.

"Gentlemen," he said, "this Negro..." He pointed to the dark-skinned prisoner. Again several times during his speech he spoke of "this Negro".

Then it was the turn of the prisoner's lawyer to talk. José de Diego, tall and good-looking, rose. "Gentlemen of the jury," he said, pointing to the prosecutor, "this red-haired Kentuckian has said..." and several other times he mentioned "this red-haired Kentuckian".

The prosecutor complained to the judge. "What has the color of my hair or the State I come from got to do with this case?"

"Exactly as much as the color of the prisoner's skin!" de Diego snapped. "Here in Puerto Rico, we do not judge a man by his color. We judge him on the evidence!"

De Diego won his case.

José de Diego y Martinez was born in 1866, the son of a Spanish army officer and a native lady. His parents died before he was twelve and his guardian, a gentleman named Santiago Sanz, sent him to Spain to a school in the city of Lagroño.

There was a bull ring near the school, and sometimes the boys were taken to see the bullfights. Perhaps Pepe (a Spanish nickname for José) dreamed of becoming a brave *torero* (bullfighter), wearing the brilliant costume, hearing the cheers of the crowd, being admired by the ladies.

If so, the dream did not last long because he was much more interested in politics and poems. When he was only fourteen he joined a local group who were trying to throw out the Spanish king and establish a republic. Even so young, he wrote a funny article that was published in a republican newspaper.

At seventeen, he was graduated from the school and went to Barcelona to study law. It was lucky that he was a bright student because he spent much of his time writing poems. With his dark good looks, he was very popular with the girls and many of his poems then were about young ladies.

But he also wrote poems and articles about politics. Many of these made fun of the king and the government. Four times the police arrested him for his writings until finally young de Diego decided he had better go home for a while and let things cool off.

In Puerto Rico, he fell deeply in love with pretty Carmita Echeverría. But her father didn't want a radical young poet for a son-in-law, and he refused them permission to marry. When de Diego felt it was safe to return to Spain in 1887 to finish his education, Carmita promised to wait for him.

But five months later, the young man learned that she was going to marry someone else. He wrote what became one of his most famous poems to express his sorrow and forgiveness. Later it turned out that she had not married the other man after all, but she was mentally ill and in an institution. For the rest of Carmita's life, de Diego sent money to the institution for her. She died in 1910.

De Diego went from Barcelona to the University of Havana in Cuba to finish his education. In 1891, now 25 years old, he came home to Puerto Rico. He joined the law firm of Rosiendo Matienzo Cintrón, a leading member of the Autonomist Party in Mayagüez. The young lawyer soon impressed other party leaders, such as Luis Muñoz Rivera and José Celso Barbosa, with his ability and sincerity.

This was the time when the Autonomists were rebuilding the party after *el Año Terrible*, and Muñoz Rivera and Barbosa were beginning to argue over whether or not they should seek the help of the Spanish Liberal Party in their struggle for freedom. De

Diego wanted independence for Puerto Rico, yet he believed that as a practical matter autonomy must come first.

He moved to Arecibo in 1894 and started an organization of Autonomists there. Also, he began to publish *La República (The Republic)*, a newspaper where he printed articles which he signed *León Americano* (American Lion). Again and again, his articles and speeches called for his island's freedom.

When Spain granted Puerto Rico the Charter of Autonomy in 1898 and Muñoz Rivera became Minister of Grace, Justice and Government, he appointed José de Diego as his second in command.

Some Puerto Ricans were not happy with the new autonomy and one of them was Aquilino Fernández Isaguirre, who had been private secretary to the evil Governor Palacio during *el Año Terrible*. Fernández was director of a newspaper, *La Unión (The Union)*, which called Muñoz Rivera a "tyrant".

De Diego challenged Fernández to a duel. They fought with swords. De Diego was wounded on the left thigh and Fernández on the right hand before the fighting was stopped.

Then came the war between the United States and Spain, and the American invasion of soldiers landing on Puerto Rico. On the evening of July 30, Muñoz Rivera and de Diego were sitting on a bench in the Plaza de Colón in San Juan when an army officer they knew, Captain Angel Rivero Mendez, came up to them.

They talked of the danger that the city might be attacked by the invading Americans. Rivero was an artillery captain stationed at *el Castillo de San Cristóbal* (the Castle of Saint Christopher) and his guns were in an exposed position. If American warships opened fire from the sea, he would very probably be killed. He told his friends this, and he advised them to leave the city.

Rivero wrote in his diary that Muñoz replied, "If it comes to that, you will stay with your cannon until death. And if it comes to that, we, too, will be at our posts." Rivero adds that de Diego agreed, the three friends embraced and all went back to duty.

Happily, the American warships did not attack the city.

De Diego stayed with Muñoz in the new military government for a little while, and then they left it together. De Diego was elected to the House of Representatives from Mayagüez in 1902 and was re-elected for the rest of his life. He became Speaker—presiding officer—in 1909.

Meanwhile, he kept on with his writing and speaking, only now his target was no longer Spain, but the United States. One of his poems says:

> The sound of war rings out.
> The Yankee threatens us,
> And wishes to be owner
> of this most beautiful island.
> Vain wish
> As long as brave heart
> Beats indignantly
> Within each Puerto Rican!
> The Nephews of Uncle Sam
> Will go home the way they came!
> Rataplán!

("Rataplán" is the Spanish word for our "rat-a-tat-tat", representing the sound of a beating drum.)

He wrote poems about the hunger and sickness of his people. Again and again he protested against American rule of the island. In 1916, he published a book of poems entitled *Cantos de Rebeldía (Songs of Rebellion)*. The first poem was called *The Last String* and it refers to the strings of a lyre, an ancient musical instrument which poets used to play while they recited or sang their poems. De Diego says that all the strings of his own lyre are broken, except one. And that one he will treasure because it is:

> A long, strong string!
> A string that's long and strong
> For the tyrant's neck!

By this time de Diego was a sick man. He had a slow-working but deadly tropical disease. In spite of that, he went to Spain to help celebrate the 300th anniversary of Miguel de Cervantes, most famous of all Spanish writers. There he was given the title of *Caballero de la Raza* (Knight of the People).

When he returned to Puerto Rico, the island doctors could give him little hope of curing his disease. Hoping to find a cure, he went to New York. The doctors there could not help him either.

De Diego died in New York on July 16, 1918.

CHAPTER XII

**HOPE MOVES THE PEOPLE**

"If I were only a giant to complete the work of Luiz Muñoz Rivera." So wrote the young Luis Muñoz Marín about his father's death. But it takes a lot of growing to make a giant, and Luis had to do that first.

He had already done much more growing than most boys of his age. Little Luis was barely three when his parents moved to New York in 1901 and so even in his very early years he learned some English and met people of different backgrounds from his own. When the family moved back to Puerto Rico, Luis went to a private school.

One of his schoolmates said, "Luis always behaved like a poet. At lunch, he would stop eating and stare into space. Sometimes he would get so absent-minded that he would scratch his head with his fork."

Luis was twelve when his father was elected Resident Commissioner and moved to Washington. At first the boy was sent to a boarding school—one where the pupils lived as well as studied. When he was filling out the entrance forms, he put down his full name, José Luis Alberto Muñoz Marín. The teacher who took the forms did not understand Spanish ways. He saw that the boy's father's last name was Rivera, so he added that to Luis' name, too. He introduced the new boy to his schoolmates as "Joe Rivera".

Later, Luis went on to Georgetown University, where he showed much more interest in writing poems, stories and essays than in his studies. During this time he lived with his father in a small apartment where the older man had the bedroom, and the son slept on the living room couch. Often they sat up late at night, talking of politics and of the problems of Puerto Rico. Through his father, Muñoz Marín met many important people in Washington and learnt the ways of that city.

When Muñoz Rivera died he left his family only $400. His friends raised enough money to buy a house in San Juan which they presented to Doña Amalia. She could live upstairs and rent the ground floor to *La Democracia* to bring in a little money.

Muñoz Marín went back to Washington for a while to work as secretary to the new Resident Commissioner. But his heart was in writing, both in Spanish and in English. By the time he was nineteen, he had published two books of his poems and essays. He tried Georgetown Law School for a year, then dropped out, and he moved to Greenwich Village in New York to make his living as a writer. He sold poems, book reviews and articles to American magazines and newspapers, not making much money, but enough to get by.

At a party he met another writer—a dark, pretty girl from Mississippi named Muna Lee. She was three years older than he and her poems, too, were being published. Six months later, they were married.

Every Sunday evening their apartment in Greenwich Village was filled with people, mostly poets and writers. Nobody was invited; they were friends who just came. Muñoz made friends with many of the most important American poets of the time—among them Edwin Markham, Vachel Lindsay, Sara Teasdale, Carl Sandburg and Archibald MacLeish. Sometimes the great Spanish bullfighter, Juan Belmonte, would come by. So sometimes did the famous explorers, Hubert Wilkins and Vilhjalmur Stefanson.

Soon after his marriage, Muñoz returned to Puerto Rico for a short visit and, to the surprise of everybody, joined the Socialist Party of Santiago Iglesias, the man with whom his father had so often disagreed but whose rights he had always defended.

Muñoz did not stay long with the Socialists. The aging Iglesias decided that the best hope for the workers of Puerto Rico was for the island to become a state and so he joined forces with his old enemies, the Conservative Republicans, to form the Coalition

Muñoz Marín and Iglesias Pantín

Party. But Muñoz was beginning to think more and more that Puerto Rico needed complete independence.

He returned to New York with Muna and with their two small children, Luisito and Munita. Doña Amalia came along to live with them.

Muñoz told the American people about Puerto Rico's poverty in an article in *The Nation* of April 8, 1925. He told about the *jíbaros*, both of how poor they were and of their good qualities as people. He told of the island's three major industries—sugar, coffee and tobacco—saying they provided all the good things that come after dinner but "without the dinner".

But in 1928 Puerto Rico was even worse off than usual. The island suffered its worse disaster of modern times. The Arawak Indians had among their gods a God of Evil named Huracan. The worst evil they knew is named for him, in English, the hurricane, most fearsome of all storms. A dreadful hurricane struck the island, killing more than 300 people, ripping the roofs off thousands of houses and carrying others away altogether. The year's crop of sugar cane was smashed. Fruit trees were blown down. Coffee plantations were completely destroyed.

There was no one to help. Earlier in the year the Puerto Ricans had written to President Calvin Coolidge telling of their problems and asking for the right to govern themselves. Coolidge wrote back that the Puerto Ricans were too ignorant and lazy because of their "moral and physical vices" to have self-government.

But in the next year, two events happened that were important to the island Theodore Roosevelt, Jr., was appointed Governor, and the United States began to slide into the Great Depression.

Roosevelt was a good and popular Governor. He studied Spanish and spoke it whenever he could. He laughed at a silly suggestion someone made. This person said that the way to help the Puerto Ricans was to give canary birds to poor people. The people would teach the birds to sing *The Star-Spangled Banner* and then sell them to tourists!

Roosevelt was much more sensible than that. He appointed as many Puerto Ricans as he could to office. He got Congress to give him $3 million for loans to small farmers, he built more schools and introduced many reforms. Muñoz Marín praised him highly, as did other islanders.

At the same time, the Depression was striking the mainland. Muñoz saw at first hand millions of men thrown out of work and people lined up for blocks to be given some bread and soup. Banks were closing and families were losing their farms and homes. The United States was free and independent, yet that fact did not save her people from poverty. Muñoz thought a great deal about this. It helped to shape his later politics.

In 1931, he and his family went home to stay. *La Democracia* hired Muñoz at a salary of $23 a week. He and his family moved into the house that Doña Amalia owned.

The paper had the first floor of the building, the Muñoz Marín family had the one above, and Doña Amalia lived on the top floor. Many an evening the second floor was filled with young people sipping coffee and talking politics, but Doña Amalia's part of the house was her own. If anyone tried to come upstairs, he would find the way blocked by a determined old lady swinging a broom at his head. "The revolution stops at the second floor," she would say.

Muñoz Marín

*La Democracia* was controlled by the Unionist Party. Its leader, Antonio Barceló, decided to change the name of the party back to the name it had used under Muñoz Rivera, the Liberals. Muñoz Marín joined it and in 1932, for the first time, he was elected to office, becoming a Senator. At the same time, Franklin D. Roosevelt was elected President of the United States.

Roosevelt made a serious mistake by appointing Robert H. Gore as Governor. Gore was a politician with no ability or understanding. He began by firing capable Puerto Ricans from important jobs and hiring his political friends instead.

He also told the men whom he was considering appointing to his Cabinet that each of them would have to give him a letter quitting his job. These letters were not to be dated. Gore's idea was than any time anyone displeased him, the Governor would simply put a date on the letter and announce that the Cabinet member had "resigned". That way he could fire anybody any time and make it seem that the person had quit on his own accord.

When this story was published in the papers, Gore said it wasn't true, and he accused Barceló of making it up. In reply, Muñoz wrote an editorial in English for a newspaper called *El Mundo (The World)*.

The headline on the editorial was, "Governor Gore, You Are a Damn Liar."

Then Muñoz went to Washington to see what he could do. There he had a good friend, Ruby Black, a newspaperwoman who often sent articles to his papers. She introduced him to President Roosevelt's wife, Eleanor. When Mrs. Roosevelt heard his story she was impressed, and asked the President to see Muñoz, which he did. Once he had heard Muñoz, President Roosevelt made Gore resign.

While he was talking to Roosevelt about Gore, Muñoz had another idea. Puerto Rico was in a bad way, even by her own standards, during the Depression. Roosevelt's New Deal was giving the island some emergency relief, but all this did was to keep some people from starving. It didn't improve conditions in the country generally. What was needed was a program that would create business and jobs in the island to get people working so they could help themselves. "We need less aspirin and more vitamins," Muñoz told the President.

Muñoz got a hero's welcome when he returned to the island, but he found problems, too. *La Democracia*, as always, had troubles. There wasn't enough money to pay all the salaries, so Muñoz suggested that the workers just split up evenly what little money there was. He wrote to a friend in New York, "You must come and work for *Democracia*. You will work like a mule, be paid like a slave and be abused like a good patriot." The friend came.

Muñoz went to his friend, Dr. Carlos Chardón, who was chancellor of the University of Puerto Rico and an expert on farming. With the help of others they drew up the Chardón Plan to bring about long-term growth for Puerto Rico. An important part of the plan aimed to break the control held by four big sugar companies over most of the island's best land. The government would take over much of the land and use it for the people. Opposed to the plan were the rich landowners and other conservative people.

Through the year 1934 the two forces battled in Congress. Finally, in December, Muñoz Marín went to Washington and made a personal appeal to President Roosevelt.

The response thrilled the entire island. On the evening of December 22 there were loudspeakers in every town square. Puerto Ricans heard the President of the United States say he had a message for them, and he then presented Muñoz Marín to read it. In Muñoz' deep voice came the words of the President: "I assure you and your people of my complete goodwill and firm determination that permanent reconstruction shall be started at the earliest possible moment on the basis of the Chardón Plan."

Again Muñoz was a hero. Congress gave $40 million to start the Puerto Rican Reconstruction Administration (PRRA), plus an extra $7.5 million from sugar taxes, in August, 1935. Yet, because of interference from Washington and political quarreling on the island, PRRA was not nearly so helpful as Muñoz had hoped.

At this time in the island there was a small group who called themselves Nationalists. Their leader was Albizú Campos. Campos had volunteered for the United States Army in World War I. Because of his dark skin he had been assigned to an all-Negro regiment and had suffered greatly from unfair treatment. As a result of this experience, he developed a bitter, undying hatred of the United States.

On Sunday morning, February 23, 1936, Colonel Francis E. Riggs came out of the Cathedral in San Juan after mass. Riggs was the island's police chief, appointed from Washington. He was an efficient policeman, but popular since he was friendly and fair.

As he walked down the Cathedral steps with his prayer book under his arm, Riggs was shot dead by two young Nationalists,

Hiram Rosado and Elias Beauchamp. The two gunmen were arrested on the spot and taken to a police station where they were both murdered.

The island was thrown into an uproar. People were sorry and ashamed about the killing of Riggs and angry about the killing of the two Nationalists. Muñoz was in Washington at the time, and he was asked by the Americans to send a statement to the Puerto Rican newspapers condemning the murder of Riggs. He said he would do it if the American authorities would also send a statement condemning the police killing of the Nationalists. This stand by Muñoz made some powerful men in Washington very angry at him.

One angry American was Senator Millard Tydings of Maryland. He introduced a bill in Congress which would have offered the Puerto Ricans a choice: either they could vote to stay with the United States or they could have complete independence immediately. But, if they chose independence they would be cut off from all connection with the United States. They would not be able to sell their sugar there because of the high tariff, and 90% of the island's income came from the sale of sugar. Given independence on those terms, Puerto Rico would starve.

The bill split the island wide open. People were either strongly for independence or strongly against it. There were strikes and disorders over the question. The Liberal Party was divided, with Barceló in favor of accepting Tydings' offer.

But Muñoz remembered something called *la Ley de Fuga* (the Law of Flight), which evil policemen sometimes used as a way of getting rid of a troublesome prisoner. You tell him he is free. Then, as he walks away, you shoot him in the back and say you had to kill him for trying to "escape". Muñoz called the Tydings Bill a *Ley de Fuga*. He still wanted independence, but he wanted it on terms that would let Puerto Rico continue to live.

Muñoz also believed that the Liberals, split as they were, would lose the 1936 elections. If they did so, he feared, the Americans would think it meant that the islanders didn't want independence. So he urged the party not to take part in the elections. But Barceló opposed him, and a party convention went along with Barceló.

The Liberals did lose the election by a close margin. Barceló blamed Muñoz for the defeat, perhaps rightly. He expelled Muñoz and his followers from the party.

It seemed as though Muñoz' political career was finished. There was no other party he could go to. There was no place to go—but to the people.

One good thing did happen to Muñoz in that dark year of 1937. He met a beautiful, black-haired, dark-eyed young schoolteacher

Institute of Culture in Old San Juan

named Inés María Mendoza de Palacios. Both were married, but their marriages were breaking up and each was separated. They became friends and worked together in the Puerto Rican cause, though they could not be married until their divorces became final some years later.

Thinking about the Tydings Bill, which did not pass Congress, about the hungry people he had seen even in the United States during the Depression, and about the hungry people in his own island, Muñoz decided that the most important thing for Puerto

Rico was not the form of her connection with the United States, her "status", but something much simpler—food and work for the people. With this in mind, he decided to build a new party—the Popular Democratic Party. "Status is not an issue," said the party. A good life for the people of Puerto Rico was what mattered first.

Very few Puerto Ricans had a decent life. The four big sugar companies owned more than half of all the best farming land. So much land was devoted to sugar that not enough land was left to grow the food the island needed. Much food had to be imported from the mainland, and then it was high-priced because of the shipping costs.

More than ten per cent of the able-bodied men had no work at all, more than five per cent only emergency relief work. Everybody had large families, so that more than forty per cent of the whole population was under fouteen years of age—a lot of hungry young mouths to feed. Many people lived in two of the ugliest slums in the world, *la Perla* (the Pearl) or else *el Fanguito* (the Little Mudhole) in San Juan, where walls were made of packing boxes, rats ran under people's feet, and the garbage smells were enough to make a person sick.

The new party had many problems. An election campaign costs money—money to buy advertising space in newspapers and radio time (today it would be television time as well), to print posters and leaflets, to supply transportation to the polling places for voters who otherwise wouldn't get there. But the party had no money.

Another problem was the sad fact that most of the *jíbaros* were used to selling their votes. On Election Day the plantation owner or a politician would give them two dollars each and tell them how to vote. Two dollars would buy a few pounds of rice and beans for hungry children. It was a lot of money to a poor man. Could the *jíbaros* be persuaded to give it up?

With a few friends in an old car, Muñoz Marín set out to go to the people in preparation for the 1940 elections. There were 786 election districts on the island and he himself spoke in more than 500 of them. Whenever his car passed two or more men beside the road, he would stop and talk to them.

At meetings he would say, "I am going to ask you an embarrassing question, and you do not have to answer unless you want to. How many of you have ever sold your votes?"

A pause. A hand would go up, then another, then some more.

"I congratulate you on your courage in telling the truth. Now tell me this. The politicians you have voted for for so many years, what did they promise you? Higher wages? Pure water? Schools for your children? Doctors?"

"Yes, yes, all those things."

"Have they done any of these things?"

"None."

"Never?"

"Never."

"But they have given you two dollars. Parties that buy elections do not need to keep their promises to the people. They take orders from those who give them the money to buy your votes.

"I ask you this: Do not give me your vote. Lend it to me. Elect me to the Senate and see if I keep my word. If, after four years, there is more food in your pot, keep Muñoz Marín and his party in office. If there is not, take back the vote you have lent and you can sell it for two dollars again.

"Remember this: you can have justice. Or you can have two dollars. But you can't have both."

All over the island Muñoz went with his message. Often there was not enough money to buy gas for the car and he would have to pass a hat around to collect a couple of dollars, a few cents at a time. Once at the town of Sabana Grande one of his friends, Raúl Gándara, had walked all over town to borrow ten dollars for gas and a meal. But as Muñoz was speaking in the town square, there rose the frightening cry of, "Fire!"

The crowd ran towards the woman who was screaming, but they could not save her little house. Within minutes, she and her children watched their home become a pile of ashes.

Muñoz went back onto the speaker's platform. "Friends," he said, "our neighbor has lost her house. Shall we all contribute to help her get a new start? Here is ten dollars . . ."

The weary Gándara went off to look for more money. If they

ate bread and cheese, and coasted down the hills to save gas, maybe five dollars would do . . .

One evening 100 of his followers were among the crowd that gathered to hear Muñoz at Guayabota de Yabucoa. After the meeting there was no place to go, but there also wasn't much of a place to sleep. The best the town could do was to find ten cots. What to do? They put two people in each cot so that 20 could sleep for a while. A *jíbaro* brought out a guitar and the rest began to dance. Every two hours, someone would wake the 20 sleepers and 20 others would take over the cots. And so it went on until dawn. The last look the people had at Muñoz was when his car started off in the morning and his head fell back as he went to sleep.

The party needed both a battle cry and a symbol that could be easily recognised by the people who could not read. Muñoz asked a friend, Antonio Colorado, to draw a symbol he had thought up. It was simple: the head of a *jíbaro* wearing a *pava*—the big straw hat of the farm workers. Under it Muñoz wrote three words: PAN—TIERRA—LIBERTAD (BREAD—LAND—LIBERTY). All over the island, the symbol appeared on posters, flags, signs.

And the slogan was equally simple: *Jalda Arriba!* —Up the Hill!

The landowners grew frightened by Muñoz' campaign. Often they tried to prevent the people from hearing him. A plantation owner in Jájome ordered the gates locked in his wire fence so the workers couldn't go out to hear Muñoz. Someone cut a hole in the fence and 200 cane cutters slipped through to go to the meeting.

Another night, as Muñoz and his friends approached Playa Cortada, they were stopped by guards with guns. The guards said they could not pass. Although the village itself was a public place, it was surrounded on three sides by private property and on the fourth side by the ocean. Muñoz was not allowed to step on the private property.

He turned to Samuel Quiñones, a lawyer friend, and asked him, "Are the streams and the sea private property?" The lawyer said they were not.

"Good," said Muñoz. "We go to Playa Cortada."

He took off his shoes and socks, rolled up his trousers and stepped into the small stream beside the road. The whole party waded to the beach, then through the water to the town square, where the rally was held.

On yet another occasion, Muñoz drove up one evening to a clearing beside the road, where he was to speak. But where was the crowd? Only two or three *jíbaros* stood there. Beyond the road, on the plantation's property, the little houses of the workers were dark and silent.

"Go ahead and talk," said one of the *jíbaros*. He pointed to Muñoz' loudspeaker. "Talk loud."

Puzzled, and feeling a little foolish at using a loudspeaker to talk to so few, Muñoz began to speak. Then he noticed a strange thing. Far behind the road, where the houses were, small lights began to appear, more and more of them, until there seemed to be hundreds of fireflies in the night air. He paused and looked at the men before him.

A man smiled. "They are not permitted to come," he explained, "so they light their candles to let you know they can hear you. Talk to them."

The Popular Democrats had drawn up a list of 24 things they would do if they were elected. But how to make people believe they would keep their promises? On the night of September 15, 1940, they held a street meeting in Santurce. While torches burned red in the night and 15,000 people watched, Muñoz led every candidate for the legislature to the platform where each man swore that he would vote for every one of the 24 points.

Just before the election the party managed to buy time for two radio broadcasts. In the first, Muñoz told the voters that no one should sell his vote, not even to the Popular Democrats. "This is not a party of animals for sale," he said, "It is a party of burdened men and women who know how to defend, as creatures of God, the justice that God wishes them to have."

And in his last broadcast, he told the people, "Let no one stop you from voting. With your votes you are working for your future. It is not a holiday; it is the most serious day of work since you were born. Better to come in clothing dirty from work than with your soul filthy from having sold your right to justice.

"And above all other things, have faith in yourselves. Believe in yourselves. Be the men and women that God wanted you to be."

When the next day was over, the *Populares* had won. Muñoz, sitting at home with a few friends, listened to the news on the radio. Suddenly a thought struck him. He who always thought of everything had forgotten something: he had made no preparations for a victory party—and he had no money to buy refreshments. Muñoz and his friends had to call up other friends to bring over food and drink for the wildly cheering crowd that filled the house.

"The sun rose on November 5, burning ropes and melting chains!" That is how Muñoz described the victory. He took some time off to rest. While he was resting, an old *jíbaro* arrived, having come down from the hills to see him. The old man said he had promised the Virgin that if Muñoz won, he would make this trip and kneel to her in Muñoz' presence.

"Let us kneel together," Muñoz said.

When the *jíbaro* was ready to leave, someone told Muñoz that the old man had sold two chickens to raise the bus fare to come, but now had no money to go home. Should they not give him the bus fare?

"When a man offers you his soul, do you give him change?" Muñoz asked. He sent the old *jíbaro* home in his own car.

The Popular Democrats' victory was not complete. Muñoz had been elected Senator by the largest vote and so was the most important man in the legislature. But of the nineteen seats in the Senate, the *Populares* had won only ten which was the barest of majorities. And of the thirty-nine seats in the House, the *Populares* had won eighteen while the conservative Coalition Party also had eighteen. The other three were held by the small Tripartite Party.

Muñoz had to make trades and deals with the Tripartites to get their votes so that he could have his bills passed. If their price was too high, he tried to get a Coalitionist or two to vote for his program. On one occasion, he counted up his support and found himself short one vote.

He went to the radio and he read again the 24 Popular points. "These are the laws the people have demanded," he said. "We are ready to pass these laws. We need only one vote. One vote!

"Where is the man who will cast this vote? *Falta un hombre!* We need one man!"

He found that man in Dr. Rafael Arrillaga Torrens, a Socialist who had been elected on the Coalition ticket. To his bitter disappointment, Dr. Arrillaga had found that the Republicans of his party were not truly interested in reforms. Only the *Populares* really were. He began to vote for the Muñoz program.

Some of the Coalitionists decided to kill Dr. Arrillaga. If a man died in office, his party could fill his place without an election, and they meant to appoint someone who would not help Muñoz.

A poor man who was dying of cancer was overhead weeping because he had no money to leave his little son. They offered him $1,000 if he would kill the doctor, and the man said he would do it. They gave him a pistol.

All day the next day the man followed Dr. Arrillaga, waiting for his chance. Towards evening, the doctor walked down a dark, empty street. The man behind him pulled out the gun.

Suddenly, out of a doorway ran a little boy, and his mother after him, both friends of the doctor. Dr. Arrillaga picked up the boy and began talking with the mother.

The would-be killer lost his nerve. He went to a bar, had many drinks and ended by getting into a fight and wounding the bartender. Then he began to cry and confessed what he had been doing.

After that, two policemen guarded the doctor wherever he went. One day, as he was driving to the Capitol building, two gunmen opened fire on his car. The doctor and his guards fired back and captured one of them. Then the doctor went on to the Capitol and voted for a bill to establish minimum wages, which passed that day.

There were still other attempts to kill him. None succeeded. Some time later, he got a letter from a man who was in prison for having tried to kill him. The man said his wife was about to have a baby, was sick and had no money. Would Dr. Arrillaga take care of her?

The doctor did.

Bill after bill, point after point, the Popular program was becoming law Muñoz was aided by the new Governor, Rexford Guy Tugwell, who, as an adviser to President Roosevelt, earlier had supported the Chardón Plan. Within a year special branches of government were set up to improve the water supply, communications, transportation, to develop industry and to handle the land problem.

The government bought many thousands of acres of land from the sugar companies. Much of it went to *jíbaros* for small farms. But because sugar is produced more efficiently on large plantations, the government kept many of them. It employed the same workers, but gave them higher wages, plus a share of the profits, forcing the sugar companies also to raise wages for their workers. The government also gave each family a little piece of land near the plantation where they could raise food for themselves.

The government then built five factories to provide jobs and supply things the island needed—cement, tile, cardboard, shoes and glass. But Muñoz found that these factories were not profitable.

A group of American businessmen offered to buy the plants. Muñoz was interested, but before the deal went through, he was approached by José Ferré Aguayo, whose family owned an iron works, a cement plant and other businesses. Luis Ferré, José's brother and head of the family, was a conservative political opponent of Muñoz.

The Ferrés also wanted to buy the plants. José argued that Puerto Ricans ought to be able to buy them if they could make as good an offer as the outsiders. Muñoz agreed. José made a good offer and it was accepted. Thus, Muñoz Marín, for reasons of principle, sold the factories to a powerful family who opposed him politically.

With the money from the sale, the government started the Puerto Rican Industrial Company, which soon came to be called *Fomento*, which means a "stirring up". At this point Muñoz remembered the old joke about the man who lifted himself up into the air by pulling on the straps of his boots. He called the whole effort to industrialize Puerto Rico "Operation Bootstrap".

Fomento, headed by a hard-driving young man named Teodoro Moscoso, set up offices in the United States and urged businessmen there to come to Puerto Rico. They wouldn't have to pay taxes for the first ten years. They would find plenty of willing workers. The new Government Development Bank would give them loans to get started. Electric power was cheap.

It began to work. Soon new plants were going up on the island and more *puertorriqueños* were taking home regular wages.

The entry of the United States into World War II helped Puerto Rico. Americans who used to drink Scotch whiskey could no longer get it and began to drink Puerto Rican rum instead. Sugar and tobacco exports increased. The federal government collected the taxes on these goods and returned the money—$160 million—to the island government.

The money built schools and health clinics. Power lines began to string out into the countryside and mountains, bringing electric light. Pure water was piped into the villages. Now for $350, plus his own work, a *jíbaro* could have a decent little house. For that sum, which could be paid in easy installments, the government would dig the foundation and supply him with the materials so that he, with the help of his family and neighbors, could finish the building.

So much was being done that at one point a newspaper reporter asked Muñoz, "Where do you go from here? "

"Wait a minute! " Muñoz replied. "We're not here yet."

So much remained to be done!

In the 1944 elections, Muñoz and the *Populares* won easily. They took 17 of the 19 Senate seats and 37 of the 39 in the House of Representatives. Now they could move their program forward even faster.

Meanwhile, Muñoz kept up the pressure on Washington for full self-government. In 1947, Congress gave in. From 1948 on, Puerto Rico would elect her own Governor.

And who else could it be but Muñoz? In the eight years of his leadership sugar workers employed by the Land Authority had earned a total of $5 million; more than 90,000 people who had been landless now had their own houses on their own plots of land; 89 new medical centers had been built; there were 2,000 new schoolrooms and 3,000 more teachers; 200,000 children were getting free school lunches; 32,000 people were moved from slums to new public housing; and electricity had been brought to 150 districts which had never had it.

Muñoz was elected by a huge majority. The largest crowd in the island's history—200,000 people—jammed San Juan to see him sworn in. At long last, after more than four centuries, the man who lived in *la Fortaleza* was Puerto Rico's own!

Improvements kept coming. Teodoro Moscoso thought the island should have a good hotel where American businessmen could stay when they came to look over possible places to build factories. He spent more than $7 million building one. People thought it was a terrible waste of government money. Some called it "Moscoso's Foolishness".

Conrad Hilton, owner of a chain of American hotels, agreed to operate it for the government. The hotel made a million dollars in its first year. Soon many others like it spread out along the beautiful beaches of San Juan. Puerto Rico is an ideal place for a holiday and, with the new air service, mainlanders could easily get there. Today the tourist business brings the island about $140 million a year.

However, Muñoz was not interested only in bringing his people more money. What, after all, is money for, if not to help a person enjoy a good life? He started something called Operation Serenity—a program designed to save the best of Puerto Rican arts, literature and culture and to give the people enjoyment in their lives.

Artists and architects cleaned up the Old City of San Juan and restored its beauty. New editions of the works of Puerto Rican poets and writers were published. Art galleries were built to house Puerto Rican paintings. Folk music was revived and recorded. Traveling companies of actors, dancers and musicians went out to the villages. "We must live like angels." Muñoz said, "and produce like the devil!"

Muñoz himself produced like the devil. He worked twelve, fourteen, sixteen hours a day and he expected others to do the same. No lazy man could last long with him. Nor was it important how much he or anybody else got paid.

Once, as he sat in the garden of *la Fortaleza* entertaining a politician from another Latin American country, a man came in and said in some embarrassment that he was there to collect Don

Luis' dues to the Popular Democratic Party. The Governor had fallen behind. He owed the party $25.

Muñoz went into the house and returned, obviously not happy. "All I have is $23," he said. "Let me pay you the rest next week."

After the man had left, the politician turned to Muñoz in astonishment: "The Governor of Puerto Rico doesn't have $25! What kind of a *latino* are you!"

Meanwhile the old argument over Puerto Rico's status continued. In 1950 Congress passed Public Law 600 which offered a compact, or agreement, with the people of the island. They could write their own constitution and organize their government in their way but, as a Commonwealth, they would keep their ties with the United States.

This idea was hated by Albizú Campos' little band of Nationalists. Campos himself was going mad. Later on doctors would say he had a form of insanity called paranoia. He ordered his followers to fight.

On October 30, 1950, two carloads of Nationalists roared up to *la Fortaleza* with guns blazing. Some were killed immediately.

President Eisenhower and Muñoz Marín

others carried on the gunfight for an hour, but they could not break inside to kill Muñoz. Nationalists also attacked other places in the island. Before the day ended, 33 persons had been killed. And two days later, two other Nationalists attempted to kill President Harry S Truman in Washington, but were themselves shot down.

The following June the people voted in favor of the Commonwealth compact. Later that year a constitutional convention met and on March 3, 1952, the voters approved the new constitution. On July 25, 1952, Governor Luis Muñoz Marín raised the new flag of the new Commonwealth.

It was 54 years to the day after General Miles had landed at Guánica.

In the 1952 elections the opposition to the *Populares* was split. The best of the old Republican group in the Coalition Party withdrew and formed a new Republican Statehood Party with the capable Luis Ferré as their candidate for Governor. The dying Socialist Party made their last try at a national election. Muñoz was re-elected overwhelmingly. Four years later he was again re-elected, though Ferré more than doubled his own votes.

As the 1960 elections approached, Muñoz could point to an astonishing record. In twenty years, production had tripled, and the income of the average family was four times as great. The people were eating three times as much milk and butter, more than twice as many eggs, almost twice as much meat. The rates of sickness and death had been greatly cut. Where formerly the average Puerto Rican could expect to live only about two-thirds as long as the average American, now he could actually expect to live longer.

Yet the gains that he had made possible were working politically against Muñoz. A whole new group of Puerto Ricans was getting more prosperous, and many of them forgot that it was the Popular reforms that had made them so and began to think more conservatively. Muñoz and the *Populares* won the 1960 elections, but for the second time the Republican Statehood Party increased its vote.

And by now there was what some called the "Muñoz Problem". In the minds of many people he had come to be, not just the head of the government, but the government itself. And the problem was, what would happen when he went? The *Populares* got tired of hearing the question, "What will you do when Muñoz dies?" Their answer was short: "We will bury him!"

Muñoz himself solved the problem. In a baseball stadium in Mayagüez, 9,000 delegates met in 1964 to nominate the Popular candidate for Governor. Muñoz rose to speak. He thanked the party for the support they had given him. Someone called out, "Long live Muñoz Marín!"

"Long live the Puerto Rican people!" the speaker shot back. "It is not Muñoz Marín, but *you—you* who have made miracles on this island. It is not my strength but yours that will keep the Puerto Rican people going up hill."

They realized that he was saying that he would not run again. The crowd broke into a tremendous roar.

"No!" they yelled. "No! *Cuatro mas! Cuatro mas!* Four more! Four more!"

Modern automobile factory illustrating growing economic development in Puerto Rico

For once in his life, the master speaker completely lost control of a crowd. Screaming women and shouting men, holding up four fingers for the four more years they wanted him to serve, completely drowned out his words.

Doña Inés jumped from her chair on the platform to take the microphone and pleaded with the crowd to let her husband talk. Finally the noise died.

Muñoz began again: "I am not leaving you. I am returning to you. I don't say good-bye to you. I go with you always."

Muñoz announced that he would run for his old office of Senator. Roberto Sánchez Vilella, who had been Secretary of State in his Cabinet, was nominated for Governor. Both were elected. Four years later, in 1968, the Republican Statehood Party elected Luis Ferré as Governor, though Muñoz remained in the Senate.

Tower of the University of Puerto Rico

As Senator and the elder statesman of the party, he could and did continue to battle for his ideals. But he could also spend more time at his beautiful house in Trujillo Alto with Doña Inés, enjoying the visits of his children and grandchildren.

Luiz Muñoz Marín devoted his whole life to fighting and working for a dream. As he said:

"We are still climbing a steep hill. We are far from the top, but we can see the top in the distance.

"I can see at the top a people well-housed, with few living in palaces, but none in poor huts or slums. I see the opportunity for honest work with enough pay for a good and satisfying life. I see families at peace in the thought that their children will be educated. I see that all of us will work with enthusiasm, in freedom and with a sense of duty and respect for the rights of others."

He had brought Puerto Rico a long way. But the battlecry was still *Jalda Arriba!*

# BIBLIOGRAPHY

Aitken, Thomas, Jr., *Poet in the Fortress*, New York, New American Library, 1964
Carreras, Carlos, N., *Hostos, Apostol de la Libertad*, Madrid, Imprenta y Litografia, 1950
de Hostos, Eugenio Carlos, ed., *Hostos, Hispanoamericanista*, Madrid, Juan Bravo, 1951
Dorvillier, William, J., *Workshop, U.S.A.: The Challenge of Puerto Rico*, New York, Coward-McCann, 1962.
Emerson, Edwin, Jr., *A History of the 19th Century Year by Year*, 3 vols., New York, P.F. Collier
Forgione, Jose D., ed., *Paginas Escogidas: Eugenio M. de Hostos (y Bonilla)*, Buenos Aires, Angel Estrada y Cia, S.A., 1952
Freire, Joaquin, *Proceres Puertorrinqueños (Tomo I)*, San Juan, Departmento de Instrucción Publica, 1966
Gruber, Ruth, *Puerto Rico: Island of Promise*, New York, Hill and Wang, 1960
Hanson, Earl Parker, *Puerto Rico: Land of Wonders*, New York, Alfred A. Knopf, 1955
Imbert, Enrique Anderson, *Historia de la Literatura Hispanoamericana*, 2 vols., Mexico, D.F., Fondo de Cultura Economica, 1954, 1967
Jay, W.M.L., *My Winter in Cuba*, New York, E.P. Dutton, 1871
Langer, William L., ed., *An Encyclopedia of World History*, Boston, Houghton Mifflin, 1940, 1952
Monclova, Lidio Cruz, *Historia de Puerto Rico, Siglo XIX, Vol. 1*, San Juan, Editorial Universitaria, Universidad de Puerto

   Rico, 1952, 1958
    *Siglo XIX, Vol. II*, 1957
    *Siglo XIX, Vol. III*, 1962
Norris, Marianna, *Father and Son for Freedom*, New York, Dodd, Mead, 1968
Office of the Commonwealth of Puerto Rico, *The Commonwealth of Puerto Rico*, Washington, D.C., Department of Labor
Pedreira, Antonio, S., *Un Hombre del Pueblo: José Celso Barbosa*, San Juan, Imprenta Venezuela, 1937
Schloat, G. Warren, Jr., *Maria and Ramon, A Girl and Boy of Puerto Rico*, New York, Alfred A. Knopf, 1966
Soler, Luis M. Diaz, *Historia de la Esclavitud Negra en Puerto Rico*, Rio Piedras, Universidad de Puerto Rico, 1965
Sterling, Philip and Maria Brau, *The Quiet Rebels*, New York, Doubleday, 1968
Tovar, Frederico Ribes, *El Libro Puertorriqueño de Nueva York*, New York, El Libro Puertorriqueño, 1968
Vivas, Jose Luis, *Historia de Puerto Rico*, Vol. III, New York, Las Americas Publishing Co., 1960, 1962

# INDEX

Acosta, José Julian, 36–37, 58–60
Aguadilla, 29, 52, 56, 103
Alcalá, Carmen, 99–100
Alcalá, Lucía, 99–100
Araujo, María Dolores, 32
Arawaks, 13, 15
Arizmendi, Bishop Juan Alejo, 25, 27
Arrillaga, Rafael, 128

Balbas, Vicente, 89–90
Baldorioty de Castro, Román, 36–42, 44–45, 61, 66, 71, 86–87, 101, 104–105
Barbosa, Belén Sanchez de, 91, 101, 103
Barbosa, Carmen Belén, 104, 108
Barbosa, Guillermo, 108
Barbosa, Hermógenes, 99
Barbosa, José Celso, 99–111
Barbosa, Manolo, 108–109
Barceló, Antonio, 119, 121–122
Beauchamp, Elias, 121
Berríos, José Escolástico, 102
Betances, Ramón Emeterio, 46–54, 56, 62, 76, 81
Black, Ruby, 119
Bonafoux, Luis, 53
Borinquén, 13
Brau, Salvador, 63

Campeche, José, 21
Campos, Albizú, 120, 132
Canovas de Castillo, Antonio, 88, 91
Carbonell, Salvador, 69
Castelar, Emilio, 61
Cepeda, Francisco, 44, 68, 70, 86–87

Chardón, Carlos, 120
Chardón Plan, 120, 128
Cintrón, Rosedo Matienza, 95, 111
Código Negro, El, 47
Coll, Marcos, 107–108
Colón, Diego, 16
Columbus, Christopher, 13, 14
Confederation of the Antilles, 53
Contreras Martinez, Juan, 70
Coolidge, Calvin, 117
Cordero, Rafael, 31–32, 34, 36
Cortabarría, Antonio, 27
Cruz, Antonio, 62
Cuban Revolutionary Committee, 90

de Diego y Martinez, José, 110–113
de León, Ponce, 14–16

El Diario, 93
*El Diario de Ponce,* 66
Echevarría, Josefa, 32
Echeverría, Carmita, 111
Egozcue, Manuel, 94

Ferdinand, King, 14
Fernandez de Cordova, Fernando, 41
Fernandez, Padre Rufo, 36
Ferré Aguayo, José, 129
Ferré Aguayo, Luis, 129, 135
Ferrer Hernández, Gabriel, 100
Fomento, 129
Foraker Act, 93, 96–97, 107

*Gabinete de Lectura Ponceño,* 67

Gándara, Raúl, 125
Garcia de Lara, José, 68
Garcia de Paredes, José, 70
Gompers, Samuel, 96
Gore, Robert H., 118–119

Henri, María del Carmen, 49
Henry, Guy V., 93
Hostos, Belinda Ayala de, 80
Hostos, Don Eugenio de, 56, 73
Hostos, Doña Maria Hilaria Bonilla de, 73
Hostos, Engracia, 74–75
Hostos, Eugenio María de, 61, 73–83

Iglesias, Santiago, 95–115
Isabella, Queen, 14

Jiménez, Simplícita, 51
Jones Bill, The, 97-98
Jones, William A., 97
Junta Electoral, 24

*La Crónica*, 66
La Democracia, 87, 94–95
La Fortaleza, 23–24, 50, 131
*La Peregrinación de Bayoán*, 75
*La Revista*, 86
*La Torre del Viejo*, 43
Lee, Muna, 115
Liberal Party, 85
*Liga de Patriotas Puertorriqueños*, 81

Maine (warship), 92
Marchesi, José Maria, 58
Marín Solá, Ramón, 42–43, 63–72
Marti, José, 45
Meléndez Bruna, Salvador, 23–24, 26, 28, 32
Messina Iglesias, Felix María de, 49–50, 64
Micault, Eduardo, 37
Miles, Nelson A., 133
Molina Vergara, Antonio, 68–69
Molinero, Paula, 32
Montes, Toribio, 64
Morro Castle, 69, 104
Moscoso, Teodoro, 129
Muñoz, Amalia Marin de, 88, 92, 96, 115–117
Muñoz, Inés, 122, 135
Muñoz Barrios, Luis, 84–98, 106

Muñoz Marin, Luis, 96, 106, 114–135
Muñoz Rivera, Luis, 71

Nadal, Ramón, 56
Nationalists, 131–133
Nuñez, Julian, 37

Operation Bootstrap, 129
Operation Serenity, 131

Padilla, José Gualberto, 35
Palacio, Romualdo, 43–44, 67–70, 86
Pi y Margall, Francisco, 39
Polanco, Juana, 32
Polo, Benito, 56
Popular Democratic Party, 123, 126–127, 130, 132
Power Giralt, José, 22
Power Giralt, Ramón, 18–30
Power Law, 29
Pressas, Epifanio, 70
Puerto Rican Reconstruction Administration (PRRA), 120
*Puerto Rico Herald,* 95

Quiñones, Francisco Mariano, 58, 60–61
Quiñones, Samuel, 125
Republican Statehood Party, 133, 135
Riggs, Francis E., 120
Rivera, Pablo, 52
Rivero Mendez, Angel, 112
Rodríguez de Tió, Lola, 18
Rojas, Manuel, 52
Roosevelt, Eleanor, 119
Roosevelt, Franklin D., 118, 128
Roosevelt, Theodore, 95
Roosevelt, Theodore Jr., 117
Rosado, Hiram, 121
Ruiz Gandia, José Antonio, 55, 57–58
Ruiz, Manuela Belvis de, 55–56
Ruiz Belvis, Segundo, 37, 49–50, 55–62

Sagasta, Práxedes Mateo, 89
Sánchez Vilella, Roberto, 135
San Juan Bautista, 14
Sanz, José Laureano, 42–64
Sísifo (Sisyphus), 92–93
Sociedad Económica de Amigos del País, 36, 40

Taft, William Howard, 96
Tapia y Rivera, Alejandro, 37
Tirado, Juan, 99–100
Tugwell, Rexford Guy, 128
Tydings, Senator Millard, 121, 123

Ulzurrum, Díez de, 67, 69
Unionist Party, 118

Vega, Carmen, 99
Vidal, Mariano, 63

Wilson, Woodrow, 97

/CT 524 T8    00001

**Library and Learning
Resources Center
Bergen Community College**
400 Paramus Road
Paramus, N.J. 07652-1595

Return Postage Guaranteed